✵ ✵ ✵

EMPOWERING *Women*

✵ ✵ ✵

BOOKS, AUDIOS, AND VIDEOS BY LOUISE L. HAY

Books
The Aids Book: Creating a Positive Approach
Colors & Numbers
Empowering Women
A Garden of Thoughts: My Affirmation Journal
Gratitude: A Way of Life (Louise and Friends)
Heal Your Body
Heart Thoughts: A Treasury of Inner Wisdom
Life! Reflections on Your Journey
Love Your Body
Love Yourself, Heal Your Life Workbook
Loving Thoughts for Health and Healing
Loving Thoughts for Increasing Prosperity
Loving Thoughts for a Perfect Day
Loving Thoughts for Loving Yourself
Meditations to Heal Your Life
101 Power Thoughts
The Power Is Within You
You Can Heal Your Life

Coloring Books/Audiocassettes for Children
Lulu and the Ant: A Message of Love
Lulu and the Dark: Conquering Fears
Lulu and Willy the Duck: Learning Mirror Work

Audiocassettes
Aids: A Positive Approach
Cancer: Discovering Your Healing Power
Elders of Excellence
Empowering Women
Feeling Fine Affirmations
Gift of the Present *with Joshua Leeds*
Heal Your Body (Audio Book)
Life! Reflections on Your Journey
Love Your Body (Audio Book)
Loving Yourself
Meditations for Personal Healing
Meditations to Heal Your Life (Audio Book)
Morning and Evening Meditations
Overcoming Fears
The Power Is Within You (Audio Book)
Self Healing
Songs of Affirmation *with Joshua Leeds*
What I Believe/Deep Relaxation
You Can Heal Your Life (Audio Book)
You Can Heal Your Life Study Course

Conversations on Living Lecture Series
Change and Transition
Dissolving Barriers
The Forgotten Child Within
How to Love Yourself
The Power of Your Spoken Word
Receiving Prosperity
Totality of Possibilities
Your Thoughts Create Your Life

Personal Power Through Imagery Series
Anger Releasing
Forgiveness/Loving the Inner Child

Subliminal Mastery Series
Feeling Fine Affirmations
Love Your Body Affirmations
Safe Driving Affirmations
Self-Esteem Affirmations
Self-Healing Affirmations
Stress-Free Affirmations

Videocassettes
Dissolving Barriers
Doors Opening: A Positive Approach to Aids
Receiving Prosperity
You Can Heal Your Life Study Course
Your Thoughts Create Your Life

EMPOWERING *Women*

Every Woman's Guide to Successful Living

Louise L. Hay

Hay House, Inc.
Carlsbad, CA

Published and distributed in the United States by:
Hay House, Inc., P.O. Box 5100, Carlsbad, CA 92018-5100
(800) 654-5126 • (800) 650-5115 (fax)

Edited by: Jill Kramer Designed by: Christy Allison

The author of this book does not dispense medical advice or prescribe the use of any technique as a form of treatment for physical or medical problems without the advice of a physician, either directly or indirectly. The intent of the author is only to offer information of a general nature to help you in your quest for emotional well-being and good health. In the event you use any of the information in this book for yourself, which is your constitutional right, the author and the publisher assume no responsibility for your actions.

Library of Congress Cataloging-in-Publication Data

Hay, Louise L.
Empowering women : every woman's guide to successful living / Louise L. Hay.
p. cm.
ISBN 1-56170-357-5 (hc)
1. Women—Psychology. 2. Self-actualization (Psychology)
I. Title.
HQ1206.H484 1997
158.1'082-dc21 96-46627
CIP

ISBN 1-56170-357-5

00 99 98 97 4 3 2 1
First Printing, January 1997

Printed in the United States of America

⁕ Contents ⁕

About *Empowering Women* xi

Introduction xiii

CHAPTER

I: *Getting Started: We Have Much to Do and Much to Learn* 1

II: *Advertising: Targeting Women's Self-Esteem* 11

III: *Choosing Positive Thoughts and Beliefs* 17

IV: *Your Relationship with...Yourself* 49

V: *Children, Parenting, and Self-Esteem* 57

VI: *Creating Your Own Good Health* 67

VII: *Exploring Sexuality* 89

VIII: *Sexual Harassment and Speaking Out* *93*

IX: *Getting Older: Improving the Quality of Your Life* 109

X: *Building a Financially Secure Future* 133

XI: *Women in Support of Women* 143

Conclusion 153

APPENDIX

Self-Help Resources 161

Recommended Reading 171

About the Author 173

* * *

Now is the time for women

to break the barriers

of self-limitation.

You can be far more

than you ever

dreamed possible.

About
EMPOWERING WOMEN

Something old, something new. This book to help women reach their true potential has some of my previous ideas and many new ideas. By reviewing the basics and adding to them, we create a firm stand for the future. Empowering women is the best thing we can do for the planet. When women are suppressed, everybody loses. When women win, we all win.

— Louise L. Hay

"Creating anything new and fresh works much better if you mindfully 'complete' what is finished at the same time that you are dreaming up the new."
— Christiane Northrup, M.D.

* Introduction *

First, please remember that all teachers are merely stepping-stones on your pathway of growth. This includes me. I am not a healer; I do not heal anyone. I am here to help you empower yourself by sharing ideas with you. I urge you to read many books and to study with many teachers, for no one person or one system can encompass it all. Life is too vast for us to totally comprehend, and Life itself is always growing and expanding and becoming more of itself. So take the best of what you read in this book. Absorb it, use it, and move on to other teachers. Continually expand and deepen your own understanding of Life.

All women, including you and me, have been shamed and blamed since childhood. We have been programmed by our parents and by society to think and behave in a certain way—to be women, with all the rules, regulations, and frustrations that come with being a woman. Some of us are very content to play that role.

Many of us are not.

Life comes in waves and learning experiences and periods of evolution. We are in a period of wonderful evolution now. For so long, women have been totally subjected to the whims and belief systems of men. We were told what we could do, when we could do it, and how. As a little girl, I remember I was taught to walk two steps behind a man and to look up to him and say, "What do I think, and what do I do?" I was not told to do this literally, but I watched my mother, and that is what she did, so that is the behavior I learned. Her background taught her to show complete obedience to men, so she accepted abuse as normal, and so did I. This is a perfect example of how we learn our patterns—accepting and repeating the behaviors and beliefs of our parents.

It took me a long time to realize that such behavior was not normal, nor was it what I as a woman deserved. As I slowly changed my own inner belief system—my consciousness—I began to create self-worth and self-esteem. At the same time, my outer world changed, and I no longer attracted men who were dominant and abusive. Inner self-worth and self-esteem are the most important things a woman can possess. If we do not have these qualities, then we need to develop them. When our self-worth is strong, we will not accept positions of inferiority and abuse. We only give in to domination from others because we accept and believe that we are "no good" or worthless.

Today I want to focus my work on helping women to become all that they can be and on helping women to truly find a place of equality in this world. I want to help see that all women have self-love, self-worth, self-esteem, and a powerful place in society. This is not to diminish men in any way, but rather to truly have "equality" between the sexes, which benefits everyone.

As you continue reading and working with this book, remember that making changes in your beliefs and attitudes takes time. How long does it take? You could ask: How quickly can we grasp and accept new ideas? It varies with each person. So don't put limitations and time limits on your progress; just do the work as best you can, and the Universe, with its unlimited knowledge, will lead you in the right direction. Step by step, moment by moment, day by day, practice will get us where we want to be.

✳ Chapter I ✳

Getting Started: We Have Much to Do and Much to Learn

I want to show you a perfect example of how women have been programmed in the past. This is an excerpt I came across from a 1950s high school home economics textbook—really!

1. *Have dinner ready.* Plan ahead, even the night before, to have a delicious meal on time. This is a way of letting him know that you have been thinking of him and are concerned about his needs. Most men are hungry when they come home, and the prospect of a good meal is part of the warm welcome they need.

2. *Prepare yourself.* Take 15 minutes to rest so that you will be refreshed when he arrives. Touch up your makeup, put a ribbon in your hair, and be fresh looking. He has just been with a lot of work-weary people. Be a little gay and a little more interesting. His boring day may need a lift.
3. *Clear away the clutter.* Make one last trip through the main part of the house just before your husband arrives, gathering up school books, toys, paper, etc. Then run a dust cloth over the tables. Your husband will feel he has reached a haven of rest and order, and it will give you a lift, too!
4. *Prepare the children.* Take a few minutes to wash the children's hands and faces (if they are small), comb their hair, and if necessary, change their clothes. They are little treasures, and he would like to see them playing the part.
5. *Minimize all noise.* At the time of his arrival, eliminate all noise of the washer, dryer, dishwasher, or vacuum. Try to encourage the children to be quiet. Be happy to see him. Greet him with a warm smile, and be glad to see him.

6. *Some don'ts:* Don't greet him with problems or complaints. Don't complain if he is late for dinner. Count this as minor compared to what he might have gone through that day. Make him comfortable. Have him lean back in a comfortable chair or suggest that he lie down in the bedroom. Have a cool or warm drink ready for him. Arrange his pillow and offer to take off his shoes. Speak in a low, soft, soothing, and pleasant voice. Allow him to relax and unwind.
7. *Listen to him:* You have a dozen things to tell him, but the moment of his arrival is not the time. Let him talk first.
8. *Make the evening his:* Never complain if he does not take you out to dinner or to other pleasant entertainment. Instead, try to understand his world of strain and pressure, his need to unwind and relax.

There is nothing wrong with any of the above IF that is what you want to do. But realize that almost all young women in those days were programmed to completely negate themselves in order to please their husbands. This was how a "good woman" was meant to behave. Great for the men, not so great for the women. We women today are the ones who must rethink our lives. We can reinvent ourselves by learning to question everything, even those things that seem quite routine: cooking, cleaning, child care, running errands, chauffeuring. All the things we have done automatically for so long need to be re-examined. Do we want to live the rest of our lives as we have done before, with just a few pieces missing as time goes by?

Building up women does not mean having to diminish men. Male bashing is as bad as female harassment. We don't want to get into that. This kind of behavior keeps us all stuck, and I feel we have had quite enough of being stuck. Blaming ourselves or men or society for all the ills in our lives does nothing to heal the situation and only keeps us powerless. Blame is always a powerless act. The best thing we can do for the men in our world is to stop being victims and get our own acts together. Everybody respects someone with self-esteem.

I have great compassion for men and the difficulties they face as they move through life. They too are stuck in their roles and carry great burdens and enormous pressures. From childhood on, little boys are taught not to cry or to express emotions. They are taught to hold in their feelings. In my opinion, that is a form of child abuse and torture. It's no wonder that as adults, men express so much anger. In addition, most men regret the lack of a good relationship with their fathers. If you want to see a man cry, give him a safe environment and get him to talk about his father. Usually so much sadness comes up as men speak of all the unsaid things between them and how they wish their childhoods might have been different. How much they wanted to hear from their fathers that they were loved and valuable.

Women as a culture have been brainwashed into believing that in order to be "good," we need to put everyone else's needs before our own. Many of us have lived our lives fulfilling the demands of what we *should* be rather than the reality of what *we are.* There are so many women who walk around in deep resentment because they feel "forced to give service" to others out of obligation. No wonder so many women are exhausted. Mothers who work usually have two full-time jobs—one at the office and another that begins after arriving home—taking care of the family. Self-sacrifice kills the one who sacrifices.

We do not have to get sick in order to get some rest. I think many dis-eases in women are a way of getting some rest time. It's the only excuse that many women will allow themselves in order to take time off. They have to be flat on their backs before they will say no.

We women need to know—really know—that we are not second-class citizens. That is a myth perpetuated by certain segments of society, and it is nonsense! The soul has no inferiority; the soul doesn't even have sexuality. We must learn to value our own lives and our own abilities as much as we have been taught to value others. I know that when the feminist movement first came about, women were so angry at the injustices that were levied upon them that they blamed men for everything. That was okay at the time. Women needed to get out their frustrations—for a while—sort of like therapy. If you go to a therapist to work out your childhood abuse, then you need to express all those feelings before you can heal.

However, when we are given the time to express those feelings, then the pendulum swings to a more balanced point. This is what is happening to women now. It is time for us to release the anger and blame, the victimhood and the powerlessness. Today it is time for us women to acknowledge and claim our own power. Now is the time for us to take our own thinking in hand and to begin to create the world of equality we say we want.

When we as women learn to take care of ourselves in a positive way, to have self-respect and self-worth, life for all human beings, including men, will have taken a quantum jump in the right direction. There will be respect and love between the sexes, and both men and women will honor each other. We will learn that there is plenty for everyone and that we can bless and prosper each other. I believe we can create a world where it is safe for us to love each other, where we can all be happy and whole.

For a long time, we women have wanted to have more dominion over our own lives. Now we have the window of opportunity to be all that we can be. Yes, there is still much inequity in the earning power and legal power of men and women. We still settle for what we can get in the courts of law. The laws were written for men. The courts talk about what a reasonable man would do, even in cases of rape!

I would like to recommend that women begin a grass roots campaign to rewrite the laws so that they are equally favorable to both men and women. We women have tremendous collective power when we get behind an issue. We need to be reminded of our power, this collective power. The amassed energy of women united in a common cause can be awesome. Seventy-five years ago, women were campaigning for their right to vote. Today, we can run for office.

I encourage women to run for political positions. We belong in politics—it is an open field for us. There are none of the restrictions of the corporate world. If we want to shape our laws and our governments so that they are equally supportive of women, then we must enter those fields. We can begin on the smallest grass roots level. We don't need a lifetime of training to enter politics. A political career is a powerful place for women.

Did you know that in 1935 Eleanor Roosevelt pushed a bill through Congress that made it a law that every new house built had to have an indoor bathroom? Many of the male members of Congress objected by saying: "How will we be able to tell the rich from the poor if everyone has bathrooms?!" Today we take indoor bathrooms so for granted that we are unaware that a powerful woman fought Congress to enact the measure. When women get it together, we will move mountains, and the world will be a better place to live.

We have come a long way, and we don't want to lose sight of that. In Colonial times, a man was the undisputed monarch of the household, and any disobedience by wife, child, or servant was punishable by whipping. In the 1850s, no respectable woman could allow herself to enjoy sex. Yes, we have come quite a distance, and we are just beginning this new phase of our evolution. We have much to do and much to learn. Women now have a new frontier of freedom, and we need new creative solutions for all women, including women who live alone.

✳ ✳ ✳

✵ Chapter II ✵

Advertising: Targeting Women's Self-Esteem

The advertising world has targeted women by taking advantage of our lack of self-esteem in order to get us to buy their products. The bottom line for most ads is, "You are not good enough...and you can only fix yourself if you buy our product." We have allowed advertisers to target us only because we believe that there is something wrong with us that needs to be fixed. We must stop buying into their attempts to make us feel inferior.

A favorite area of attack by advertisers is our bodies. Due to the negative beliefs about our bodies that we have accepted from society and through the heavy barrage of "you're not good enough" advertising aimed at women, it is no wonder that most of the time we do not love our bodies. How many of us can really say that we love our rectums? We have enough trouble trying to accept our noses and hips. I wonder at what age we learn to equate our self-worth with our bodies. Babies never feel that they are not good enough because of the size of their hips!

As vulnerable teenage girls, we are bombarded with advertising that tries to bring down our self-esteem and to get us to feel that we need this certain product in order to be attractive or accepted by others. That is why teenage girls in our society, as a group, have the lowest self-esteem. This diminished sense of self-esteem then continues on into our adult years, in many cases. The tobacco companies love to target teenage girls with their advertising because these companies know that if you take people with low self-worth and make them addicts, then you have a good chance of creating customers for life. How can we allow them to do this to our children?

I heard a three-year-old girl say the other day, "I don't want to wear this dress; it makes me look fat." Ten-year-old girls are dieting.

We have anorexia and bulimia running rampant in our schools. What are we doing to our children? If you are a parent, do show your children how the advertisements are exploiting them. Dissect ads together. Let your children show you what is manipulative in the ads. Teach them early, and give them the power to live their lives through intelligent choices, to act rather than react.

Have you noticed how many women's magazines run the latest diets AND recipes for fattening desserts in the same issue? What kind of messages are they giving us? Fatten up, slim down, fatten up, slim down. No wonder so many women are into yo-yo dieting. There is no way we can live up to every advertisement and media message that comes along. Next time you see an ad in a magazine or on TV, look at it critically. What is the real message that advertisers are giving you? Are they trying to make you feel inferior or not good enough? Are they showing you an impossible dream to live up to? Beginning to laugh at the ads you see no longer gives them power over you. Exploitative ads are another way of controlling and dominating women. We want to do everything we can to take our power back.

I would like to see a campaign started where every time we see an ad in a magazine or a TV commercial that really insults the intelligence of women, instead of looking at ourselves and saying, "If only my hips looked like hers," or whatever, that we sit down and send a postcard to the company and say: "How dare you try to exploit me. I will never buy your product again!" If we women would send postcards to the negative, manipulative advertisers and only buy products from the companies that support women in their advertising, then the ads will begin to change.

We buy so many things just because we feel, "Oh, if I only had that, I'd be okay." Yet our thoughts come back again to the old belief: "We are not good enough. We are not good enough." We need to know, *really know*, that we women are good enough EXACTLY the way we are.

Get together with a group of friends and go through any woman's magazine. Examine the articles and the ads. Become aware of what you are looking at and what the subliminal messages are. We women need to open our eyes. We need to open our ears. What is really being shown? What is really being said? How are advertisers trying to control us?

Let's really give this issue some thought!

✳ Chapter III ✳

Choosing Positive Thoughts and Beliefs

As many of you know, my belief is that the thoughts we think, the words we speak, and the beliefs we hold are very powerful. They shape our experiences and our lives. It is almost as if every time we think a thought or speak a word, the Universe is listening and responding to us. So if there is something in our life that we do not like, then we have the power to make changes. We have the power of our thoughts and words. As we change our thinking and our words, our experiences also change. No matter where we came from, no matter how difficult our childhood was, we can make positive changes today. This is a powerful, liberating concept, and as we believe it, it becomes true for us. To me, this is how we address all issues first. We first make the changes in our minds, and then life responds to us accordingly.

What we are always doing is living our past. What we are living in this moment is what we have created from our past thoughts and beliefs. So if there is something going on in our lives that we don't like, we have the option of re-creating our experiences for the future. As we begin to change our thinking, we may not see many positive results right away, but as we continue with our new thought patterns, we will find our tomorrows becoming different. If we want our tomorrows to be positive, then we must change our thinking today. Today's thoughts create tomorrow's experiences.

Many people ask me: "How can I think positively when I'm always around negative people?" When I'm around people who are saying negative things, I say silently to myself, "It may be true for you, but it's not true for me." Sometimes I will even say it out loud. This outlook gives other people permission to be as negative as they want while I hold true to my own positive beliefs. I do my best to avoid people like that. You might ask yourself why you are *always* around negative people. Remember that we cannot change anyone else. We can only change ourselves. When we change inside, then other people will react to that change. The most important thing we can do is to change our thinking patterns. I don't care how busy we are or how hard we work, we're still thinking, and nobody can get into our thoughts.

I would like us all to put the word *neuropeptides* into our vocabulary. This word, coined by Candace Pert in her research on brain function, refers to the "chemical messengers" that travel throughout the body whenever we think a thought or speak a word. When our thoughts are angry, judgmental, or critical, the chemicals they produce depress our immune system. When our thoughts are loving, empowering, and positive, the messengers carry other chemicals to enhance the immune system. Science is finally agreeing with what many of us have known for years—that there is a body/mind connection. This communication between the mind and body never sleeps. Your mind is constantly relaying your thoughts to the cells in your body.

So moment by moment, we are consciously or unconsciously choosing healthy thoughts or unhealthy thoughts. These thoughts affect our bodies. One thought by itself does not have much influence over us. However, we all think over 60,000 thoughts a day, and the effect of our thoughts is cumulative. Poisonous thoughts poison our bodies. Science is now confirming that we cannot allow ourselves to indulge in negative thinking. It is making us sick and killing us.

For a long time, I did not understand the expression: "We are all one; we are created equally." It did not make sense. I could see that there are rich and poor, beautiful and unattractive, brilliant and stupid, every color, every race, unlimited religions and ways of looking at life. There seemed to be so many differences between people. How could we say they were all created equally?

Finally, my understanding grew, and I learned what it meant. I credit author/lecturer Caroline Myss with this new level of comprehension. You see, the thoughts we think and the words we speak affect ALL of our bodies equally. The neuropeptides, the chemical messengers that travel throughout our bodies every time we think a thought or speak a word, affect us ALL IN THE SAME WAY. A negative thought is as toxic to an American body as it is to a Chinese body or an Italian body. Anger is as toxic within a Christian person as a Jewish person or Muslim person. Men, women, homosexuals, heterosexuals, children, the elderly—all react EQUALLY to the neuropeptides created by our thinking processes.

Forgiveness and love are healing to us all, no matter what country we live in. All of the individuals on this planet need to heal their spirits before they can have permanent healings in their bodies. We come here to learn the lessons of forgiveness and self-love. Nobody, no matter where they live, will escape these lessons. Are you fighting your lessons, insisting on being self-righteous and bitter? Are you willing to learn to forgive others and yourself? Are you willing to love yourself and to move on into the richness and fullness of Life? These are the lessons of Life, and they affect us all *equally*. We are all One. We are all created equally. LOVE HEALS US

ALL! (For those of you who are ready to work on a deeper spiritual level, I urge you to read *Anatomy of the Spirit: The Seven Stages of Power and Healing*, by Caroline Myss, Ph.D. Her information is phenomenal.)

So, what kind of thoughts are you having right now? What kind of neuropeptides are traveling through your body right now? Is your thinking making you sick or well?

Far too many of us sit in our own self-created prison of self-righteous indignation/ resentment. What we have not understood is that blame creates more havoc for the blamer than for the blamed. The neuropeptides that carry the blame thoughts throughout the body slowly poison our cells.

Let us also be clear that our ego self always wants to keep us enslaved and unhappy. The ego is the voice within that will always tell us to have "one more bite, take one more drink, smoke one more joint, do it just one more time." But we are not our bodies, we are not our thoughts, and we are not our egos. We own our bodies. We are the thinker that thinks the thoughts. When our self-worth and self-esteem are strong, we will never give in to the voice of the ego. We are far more than we think we are.

Right now I want you to get up. Take this book with you, and find a mirror. Look into your eyes, and say to yourself out loud: *"I love you, and I am beginning to make positive changes in my life right now. Day by day I will improve the quality of my life. It is safe for me to be happy and fulfilled."* Say this three or four times. Breathe in between. Notice what thoughts are running rampant in your mind as you make this positive affirmation. That is just old chatter. Say to it: "Thank you for sharing." You can acknowledge the negative thoughts without giving them power. From now on, every time you see a mirror, I want you to look in your eyes and say something positive to yourself. If you are in a hurry, just say "I love you." This simple exercise will produce great results in your life. If you don't believe me, just try it.

The Answers Are Within Us

It is crucial that we always keep in mind that what we think and say becomes our experiences. As such, we will pay attention to our thoughts and speaking patterns so that we may shape our lives in accordance with our dreams. We may say wistfully, "Oh, I wish I could have or would have, or that I could be or would be...," but we don't seem to use the words and thoughts that can actually make those wishes a reality. Instead, we visualize the worst. We think every negative thought we know and then wonder why our lives are not working in the way that we would like.

We want to find our Inner Resources and our Universal Connection—that Great Central Source of all life. We want to find and use our Inner Core. We all have a treasure trove of wisdom, peace, love, and joy inside of us. And they are only a breath away. I believe that within each of us is an *infinite* well of peace, joy, love, and wisdom. When I say it is only a breath away, I mean that all we have to do to connect with these places is to close our eyes, take a deep breath, and say to ourselves, *"I now go to that place within me where there is infinite wisdom; the answers I seek are within me."*

All the answers to all the questions we will ever ask are already within us. We just need to take the time to connect. That's the value and importance of meditation. It quiets us down so that we can hear our own inner wisdom. Our inner wisdom is the best direct connection we have with all of Life. We do not need to chase after those gifts of Inner Wisdom. We just need to create the opportunity for them to come to us. And how do we do that? We can take the time to sit quietly, to go within, and find peace, deep and serene as a mountain pool. In meditation we can find joy. We can connect with an infinite well of love. It is all there within us. And nobody can take these treasures from us.

We are meant to explore new depths within ourselves and to make new decisions on how we want to live our lives. We as women have been programmed to accept limited choices. Many married women are extremely lonely because they feel they have lost their choices. They have given their power away. They do what I used to do—they look to a man for all the answers, instead of going within. In order to have change in our lives, we first need to make these new choices in our minds. We change our own thinking, and then the outer world responds to us differently.

So, I am asking you to go within and be willing to change your thinking. Connect with the treasures within you, and use them. When we connect with the treasures within, then we will give to life from the magnificence of our being. Connect with your treasures every day.

It is vital that we give ourselves the time to listen to our inner wisdom. No person can be totally in touch with the abundance of knowledge within without taking time each day to meditate. Sitting in silence is one of the most valuable things we can do. No one out there knows more about our life, or what is best for us, than we do, right here inside. Listen to your own voice. It will always steer you through life in the best possible way for you!

Let's all create a rich inner space. Let your thoughts be your own best friends. Most people think the same thoughts over and over. Remember, we think an average of 60,000 thoughts a day, and most of them are the same thoughts we had the day before and the day before that. Our thinking can become ruts of negativity or foundations to a new life. Think new thoughts every day. Think creative thoughts. Think of new ways to do old things.

Our consciousness is like a garden. Whether it is the garden around our house, or the garden of our minds, the most important first step is building good soil. You begin by getting out all the weeds, all the rocks, all the debris that you can find. You add compost and amendments and mix it well. Then when you plant, the vegetation will grow quickly and beautifully. It's the same thing with our minds. If you want your affirmations to grow quickly, then begin by removing every negative thought and belief you can find. Then you plant some good beliefs, some really good, positive thoughts. You affirm what you want to have in life, and there will be nothing to stop you. Your garden of thoughts will grow most abundantly.

Overcoming Fear

Because of the way women are raised, to be caretakers and servers, to put others' needs first, most of us do not have enough self-esteem and self-worth. We have great fears of abandonment. We fear loss and lack of security. We were not raised to believe that we could take care of ourselves. We were taught to only take care of others. When women get divorced, they are terrified. If they have young children, it is worse. They ask themselves over and over, "How will I ever make it on my own?"

We also stay in terrible jobs and marriages

because we are so terrified of being on our own. Many women don't believe that they are good enough. They don't believe that they can take care of themselves, and yet they *can.*

For many women, there is a great fear of being successful. They do not believe that they deserve to feel good or to be prosperous. When you always put yourself second, it is hard to feel deserving. Many women are frightened to be more successful or earn more money than their fathers did.

So how do we overcome fear of abandonment or the fear of success? They are two sides of the same coin. It is in learning to trust the process of Life itself. Life is here to support us, to lead us and guide us *if* we will allow it to do so. If we were raised with guilt and manipulation, then we always feel "not good enough." If we were raised to believe that life is difficult and frightening, then we don't know how to relax and let Life take care of us. We read the newspapers and see all the crime on TV, and we believe that the world is out to get us. But we all live under the law of our own consciousness—that is: what we believe, becomes true for us. What is true for someone else does not have to be true for us. If we only buy into society's negative beliefs, then these expectations will be true for us, and we will have many negative experiences.

However, as we learn to love ourselves, as our thinking changes, as we develop self-worth and self-esteem, then we begin to allow Life to bring to us all the good it has in store. This may sound simplistic, and it is. It is also true. When we relax and allow ourselves to believe: "Life is here to take care of me, and I am safe," then we begin to flow *with* Life. Begin to notice synchronistic things in your life. When you get the green light or the great parking place, when someone brings you exactly what you need, when you hear that bit of information you wanted, say "THANK YOU!" The Universe loves a grateful person. The more you thank Life, the more Life will give you to be thankful for.

I truly believe that I am Divinely protected, that only good can come into my life and that I am safe. I know that I am good enough and that I deserve all good. It has taken me many years and much study to get to this place. I had truckloads of negatives to release. I have gone from being a bitter, fearful, poor, negative woman to being a woman of confidence who shares in the abundance of Life. If I can do it, you can, too—if, that is, you are willing to change your thinking.

If only we all knew that each of us always has two guardian angels with us. These angels are here to help us and guide us, but we must ask for this help. They love us very much and await our invitation. Learn to connect with your angels, and you will never feel alone again. Some women can see their angels, some can feel them, some hear their voices, some sense their names. I call my two angels "Guys." I sense them as a pair. When there is an issue I don't know how to handle, I turn it over to them. "You handle it, Guys. I don't know what to do." When good things happen, when synchronistic things happen in my life, I immediately say "Thanks, Guys, that was great, you really did a good one this time. I really appreciate it." Angels, too, love gratitude and appreciation. Do make use of them—that is why they are with you. Angels love to be helpful!

To begin to connect with your own personal angels, sit quietly, close your eyes, take a few deep breaths, and try to sense their presence just behind your shoulders, one on either side. Feel their love and warmth. Ask them to show themselves to you. Allow yourself to experience their protection. Ask them for help with some problem, or for the answer to a question you have. You may feel an immediate connection, or you may need to practice for a while. But let me assure you: they are there, and they love you. There is nothing to fear.

Recognizing Our Beliefs

Now let's look at how we can release or change our negative beliefs. First, we have to identify the negative belief. Most of us do not have the faintest idea *what* it is that we do believe. Once we have recognized the negative belief, then we can decide if we want this belief to continue to create our circumstances.

The quickest way to discover what your beliefs are is to make lists. Start with several large pieces of paper. At the top of each page, write: WHAT I BELIEVE ABOUT: (men, work, money, marriage, love, health, aging, death), and so on. Write this statement with respect to any subject that has meaning in your life. Use a separate piece of paper for each subject. Then begin to list the thoughts that come up when you write those statements. You won't do this exercise in two minutes. It takes time. You can work on it for a few minutes every day. Write down whatever thought comes up, no matter how foolish it may seem. Just write it down. These beliefs are the internal, subconscious rules you live your life by. You cannot make positive changes in your life until you can recognize the negative beliefs you hold. By becoming self-aware, you can remake yourself at any time and become the person you want to be and live the life you dream about.

When the lists are more or less completed, read them over. Mark with a star each belief that is nourishing and supportive of you. Those are the beliefs you want to keep and reinforce. Use a different-color pen to check off each belief that is negative and detrimental to your goals. These are the beliefs that have been holding you back from being all that you can be. These are the beliefs that you want to erase and reprogram.

Look at each negative belief and ask yourself: "Do I want this belief to continue to run my life? Am I willing to let this belief go?" If you are willing to change, then make a new list. Take each negative affirmation (all beliefs are affirmations), and turn it into a positive declaration for your life. For instance: "My relationships with men are a disaster" could turn into "Men love and respect me." "I will never amount to anything" becomes "I am a confident, accomplished woman." "I don't know how to find a good job" turns into "Life brings me the perfect job." "I go from one illness to another" is transformed into "I am a big, strong, healthy woman." These examples are from my own experience. You too can take each negative belief you have and transform it into a new personal law for yourself. Create the guidelines you want to have for your life. Turn each negative into a positive. Read these positive statements out loud to yourself each day. Do them in front of a mirror—they will become true quicker. Mirrors are magical for declaring your affirmations.

Affirmations: Providing a New Direction in Life

Affirmations must always be in the present tense. Say "I have" or "I am" instead of "I will have" or "I want to be." When affirmations are spoken in the future tense, then the results stay "out there" just beyond our reach.

Very often we do not take time in our busy schedules to work on ourselves. A good way to make time for inner work is to get together with a friend or a few friends and create a little study group. One afternoon or evening a week can be set aside for this purpose. Make your lists together. Help each other with affirmations. Perhaps discuss the rest of this book. A few weeks of exploring ideas together can accomplish miracles. You will learn from each other. Collective energy is very powerful. All you need is a notebook, a mirror, a big box of tissues, and a loving, open heart. I guarantee that no matter what size the group is, you will each become more aware of who you are, and you will improve the quality of your life.

Let's ask ourselves a few questions. When answered honestly, our replies can give us a new direction in life:

* How can I take this time to make my life the best it can be?
* What are the things I want from a mate?

- What are the things I believe I need to get from a mate?
- What is it I can do to fulfill these areas? (Don't expect a mate to do everything for you. That's a terrible burden for him or her.)
- What would fulfill me? And how can I give it to myself?
- What is my excuse when I have no one to put me down?
- If I never had a mate in my life again, would I destroy myself over that lack? Or would I create a wonderful life and become a shining beacon for other women? A wayshower (someone who shows the way)!
- What have I come to learn? What have I come to teach?
- How can I cooperate with Life?

It is time for all of us to develop our own philosophy of life and to create our own personal laws—statements that we can live by, beliefs that nourish and support us. This is the set of laws that I have developed for myself over a period of time:

* *I am always safe and divinely protected.*
* *Everything I need to know is revealed to me.*
* *Everything I need comes to me in the perfect time/space sequence.*
* *Life is a joy and filled with love.*
* *I am loving and loved.*
* *I am vibrantly healthy.*
* *I prosper wherever I turn.*
* *I am willing to change and grow.*
* *All is well in my world.*

I repeat these statements often. I often begin and end my day with them. I will say them over and over if something goes wrong in any area. For instance, if I feel under the weather, then I repeat: "I am vibrantly healthy" until I feel better. If I walk in a dark area, I will repeatedly affirm: "I am always safe and Divinely protected." These beliefs are so much a part of me that I can turn to them in an instant. I suggest that you make a list that reflects your philosophy of life today. You can always change it or add to it. Create your new personal laws now. Create a safe universe for yourself. The only power that could harm your body or your environment would be your own thoughts and beliefs. These thoughts and beliefs are changeable.

Like everyone else in life, I, too have problems and crises. This is the way I have learned to handle them. The moment a problem comes up, I immediately say:

> *"All is well. Everything is working out for my highest good. Out of this situation only good will come. I am safe."*

Or:

> *"All is well. Everything is working out for the highest good for everyone concerned. Out of this experience only good will come. We are safe."*

I will repeat a variation of one of these statements over and over again, maybe nonstop for 20 minutes or so. Within a short period of time, either my mind will clear and I will see the situation differently, or I will have a solution, or the phone will ring and something has shifted and changed. Sometimes when we get over the panic of a situation, we may find that the change really is better than what was originally planned. Sometimes the way we try to control our experiences is not what is best for us.

Using this attitude and affirmation now works every time for me. I pull away from the problem and affirm the truth about myself and about my life. I get my "worry mind" out of the way so that the Universe can find a solution. I have used it in traffic jams, at airports, with relationships, with health problems, and with work issues. This is learning to flow with life, rather than fighting every change in plans. Let this be your "new" reaction to problems, and watch them disappear.

Learning and growing is all part of our soul's evolution. Every time we learn something new, we deepen our understanding of Life. There is so much to Life that we have not yet learned. We still have 90 percent of our own brain to explore and use. I believe that this is the most exciting time to be alive. I thank Life every morning when I wake up for the privilege of being here and experiencing all that is. It is part of my five or ten minutes of gratitude, beginning with thanking my bed for a good night's sleep. I express gratitude for my body, my home, my animals, my friends, the material things I possess, and all the wonderful experiences I know I will have during the day. I always end by asking Life to give me more understanding to increase my understanding so that I may continually see the larger picture. For when we see and know more, Life becomes simpler. I trust my future to be good.

Remember: Affirmations are positive statements that consciously reprogram your mind to accept new ways of living. Choose affirmations that empower you as a woman. Every day, affirm at least a few of these:

Affirmations for Women

I claim my feminine power now.
I am discovering how wonderful I am.
I see within myself a magnificent being.
I am wise and beautiful.
I love what I see in me.
I choose to love and enjoy myself.
I am my own woman.
I am in charge of my life.
I expand my capabilities.
I am free to be all that I can be.

I have a great life.
My life is filled with love.
The love in my life begins with me.
I have dominion over my life.
I am a powerful woman.
I am worthy of love and respect.
I am subject to no one; I am free.
I am willing to learn new ways of living.
I stand on my own two feet.
I accept and use my own power.
I am at peace with being single.
I rejoice and enjoy where I am.
I love and enjoy myself.
I love, support, and enjoy the women in my life.
I am deeply fulfilled by life.
I explore all the many avenues of love.
I love being a woman.
I love being alive at this point in time and space.
I fill my life with love.
I accept my gift of this alone time.
I feel totally complete and whole.
I give myself what I need.
It is safe for me to grow.
I am safe, and all is well in my world.

A Healing Meditation

I am willing to see the magnificence of me. I now choose to eliminate from my mind and life every negative, destructive, fearful idea and thought that would keep me from being the magnificent woman that I am meant to be. I now stand up on my own two feet and support myself and think for myself. I give myself what I need. It is safe for me to grow. The more I fulfill myself, the more people love me. I join the ranks of women healing other women. I am a blessing to the planet. My future is bright and beautiful.

And so it is!

Remember: The smallest positive change in your thinking can begin to unravel the biggest problem. When you ask the right questions of Life, Life will answer.

There are many ways to make our changes. We could also begin to honestly look at our flaws—NOT by looking at what is WRONG with us, but to see the barriers that we have put up that keep us from being all that we can be. And without self-bashing, we eliminate these barriers and make changes. Yes, many of those barriers are things we learned in childhood. They never were true for us. We merely accepted someone else's belief system. If we learned these thoughts once, then we can now unlearn them. We acknowledge that we are willing to learn to love ourselves. And then we develop a few guidelines:

1. **STOP ALL CRITICISM.**

   It is a useless act; it never accomplishes anything positive. Don't criticize yourself; lift that burden from yourself. Don't criticize others either, as the faults we usually find in others are merely projections of the things we don't like in ourselves. Thinking negatively about another person is one of the greatest causes of limitation in our own life. Only *we* judge ourselves, not Life, not God, not the Universe.

   I love and approve of myself.

2. **DON'T SCARE YOURSELF.**

   We all want to stop that. Too often we terrorize ourselves with our own thoughts. We can only think one thought at a time. Let's learn to think in positive affirmations. In this way, our thinking will change our lives for the better. If you catch yourself scaring yourself again, immediately say:

I release the need to scare myself. I am a divine, magnificent expression of life, and I am living fully from this moment on.

3. BE COMMITTED TO THE RELATIONSHIP YOU HAVE WITH YOURSELF.

We get so committed to other relationships, but we sort of toss ourselves away. We get around to ourselves only now and then. So, really care for who you are. Be committed to loving yourself. Take care of your heart and soul.

I am my favorite person.

4. TREAT YOURSELF AS THOUGH YOU ARE LOVED.

Respect and cherish yourself. As you love yourself, you will be more open to love from others. The Law of Love requires that you focus your attention on what you *do* want, rather than what you *don't* want. Focus on loving *you.*

I love myself totally in this moment.

5. TAKE CARE OF YOUR BODY.

Your body is a precious temple. If you are going to live a long, fulfilling life, then you want to take care of yourself now. You want to look good, and most of all, feel good with lots of energy. Nutrition and exercise are important. You want to keep your body flexible and moving easily until your last day on the planet.

I am healthy, happy, and whole.

6. EDUCATE YOURSELF.

Too often we complain that we don't know this or that, and we don't know what to do. But we are bright and smart, and we can learn. There are books and classes and tapes everywhere. If money is a consideration, then use the library. Find a self-help group—they are listed under Community Services in the yellow pages of the telephone book. I know I shall be learning until my very last day.

I am always learning and growing.

7. BUILD A FINANCIAL FUTURE FOR YOURSELF.

Every woman has a right to have money of her own. This is a significant belief for us to accept. It is part of our self-worth. We can always start on a small level. The important thing is that we keep saving. Affirmations are good to use here.

I am constantly increasing my income.
I prosper wherever I turn.

8. FULFILL YOUR CREATIVE SIDE.

Creativity can be any activity that fulfills you. It can be anything from baking a pie to designing a building. Give yourself some time to express yourself. If you have children and time is short, find a friend who will help you take care of your children, and vice versa. You both deserve time for yourselves. You are worth it.

Affirm:

I always find time to be creative.

9. MAKE JOY AND HAPPINESS THE CENTER OF YOUR WORLD.

Joy and happiness are always within you. Make sure you are connected with this place inside of you. Build your life around this joy. When we are happy, we can be creative, we don't sweat the small stuff, and we are open to new ideas. A good affirmation to use often is:

I am filled with joy, and I express happiness.

10. HAVE INTEGRITY; KEEP YOUR WORD.

In order to honor and respect yourself, you must have integrity. Learn to keep your word. Do not make a promise you will not keep—even to yourself. Don't promise yourself you will start the diet tomorrow or exercise every day *unless* you know you will follow through. You want to be able to trust yourself.

11. DEVELOP A STRONG SPIRITUAL CONNECTION WITH LIFE.

This connection may or may not have anything to do with the religion we were raised in. As children, we had no choice. Now as adults, we can choose our own spiritual pathway and beliefs. Solitude is one of the special times in one's life. Your relationship with your inner self is the most important one. Give yourself quiet time, and connect with your inner guidance.

My spiritual beliefs support me and help me be all that I can be.

We want to take these ideas and reaffirm them—until they are firmly in our consciousness, and they are a part of our lives!

✳ Chapter IV ✳

Your Relationship with...Yourself

In this section of the book, rather than focusing on how you can be more fulfilled in your current relationships or how to find the perfect mate (subjects about which there have been dozens of books already written), I would like to concentrate, instead, on the most important relationship in your life—the relationship you have with *yourself.*

Many women get hung up on the question: "How can I fulfill myself without a mate?" This can be a frightening concept for many women. We need to acknowledge our fears and walk through them. Make a list of all your fears (WHAT I AM AFRAID OF...), look at them closely, and then begin to dissolve them. You don't have to fight them; that gives them too much power. Do a meditation where you look at each fear and then drop it in a stream of water to literally dissolve it and make it disappear downstream. Then turn each of those fears into positive affirmations. "I am afraid that no one will ever love me" can become "I am someone, and I love myself deeply and truly." If we can't give ourselves the love we say we want, then we will never find it in the outer world. Don't waste time longing for something that is not in your life at the moment. Begin by being tender and loving to *you*. Let your body and your heart experience what love *feels* like. Treat yourself the way you want a lover to treat you.

Almost every woman lives alone at some point in her life—either as a young single, a divorced woman, or as a widow. I think ALL women, even those in wonderful relationships at the present time, need to ask themselves the question: "Am I prepared to live by myself?" To totally depend on other people to take care of us is not being in touch with our own inner resources. Even when we're in a relationship, we all need to have time alone—

time to find out who we are, and time to think about goals and the changes we would like to make for ourselves. Our alone time can be just as fulfilling as the time we spend with other people—especially if we make our thoughts our own best friends.

Today, an unmarried woman has the whole world in front of her. She can rise as high as her capabilities and her belief in herself. She can travel, choose her jobs, make good money, have lots of friends, and develop great self-esteem. She can even have sexual partners and loving relationships if she wants them. Today, a woman can choose to have a baby without having a husband and still be socially acceptable, as many of our well-known actresses and other public figures are doing. Today's woman can create her own lifestyle.

For many women around the world, there may never be a long-lasting relationship with a man. They could be single for the rest of their lives. At the moment, in the United States there are approximately 122 million men and 129 million women. The gap is even wider in some other countries, including France. Singlehood is growing as never before. We do not want to view this statistic as a tragedy. We want to see it as an opportunity for the evolution of women. You know how it often is in your own life—when you don't make the changes you need to make, life will often take a hand and force you to make the change. For instance, you don't leave the job you hate, then they end up FIRING you. Life gives you the opportunity you wouldn't take for yourself. Women have not made the positive changes in consciousness necessary to be fulfilled and empowered, and now life has taken a hand.

We All Have Love Within Us

It is sad that so many women continue to moan and cry if they don't have a man by their side. We don't need to feel incomplete if we are not married or not in a relationship. When we "look for love," we are saying that we don't have it. But we all have love within us. No one can ever give us the love we can give ourselves. Once we give our love to ourselves, no one can ever take it from us. We want to stop "looking for love in all the wrong places." Being addicted to finding a partner is as unhealthy as remaining in an addictive or dysfunctional relationship. If we are addicted to finding a partner, then this addiction only reflects our feelings of lack. It is as unhealthy as any other addiction. It's another way of asking, "What's wrong with me?"

There is much fear surrounding "being addicted to finding a partner"—and many feelings of "not being good enough." We have put so much pressure on ourselves to find a partner that far too many women settle for unfulfilling or even abusive relationships. We don't have to do this to ourselves. It is not an act of self-love.

We don't need to create pain and suffering for ourselves, nor do we need to feel acutely lonely and unhappy. These are all choices, and we can make "new choices" that support and fulfill us. Granted, we have been programmed to accept limited choices. But that was in the past. We want to remember that this is a new day, and the point of power is always in the present moment. What we choose to believe and accept today will create our future. We can change our thinking and our beliefs. We can begin right now, in this moment, to create new horizons for ourselves. We want to be able to see our time alone as a gift!

Sometimes it is better for us to be alone. More and more women who have completed one marriage (either through divorce or widowhood), and can support themselves, are choosing not to remarry. Marriage is a custom that primarily benefits men. They see marriage as entering servitude and losing their independence. We women have been taught to deny ourselves for the sake of the marriage, and men believe that marriage is there to support them. Rather than losing their independence, many women are choosing to remain single. Being obedient to a man no longer appeals to them.

There is an old proverb that says: "Women hold up half the sky." It's time we make that true. We will not learn how, though, by whining, by being angry, by making ourselves the victims, or by giving our own power away to men or to the system. The men in our lives are mirrors of what we believe about ourselves. So often we look to others to make us feel loved and connected when all they can do is mirror our own relationship with ourselves. We really need to improve the relationship we have with ourselves in order to move forward. I would like to concentrate most of my own work on helping women "accept and use" their own power in the most positive ways.

We all need to be very clear that the love in our lives begins with us. So often we look for "Mr. Right" to solve all our problems, in the form of our fathers, our boyfriends, our husbands. Now is the time to be "Ms. Right" for ourselves. If I do not have Mr. Right in my life at the moment, I can still be Ms. Right for myself. I can take control of my life and create the kind of life I want to have.

So if you are not in a relationship, don't think you are *doomed* to be alone. Think of it as an opportunity to create a life for yourself that you never dreamed possible. As a child and even as a young woman, I could never have envisioned the life that I have now. Love yourself and let Life lead you where you are meant to go. All the barriers are down. We can fly as high as we want to.

✴ Chapter V ✴

"As long as we have to 'beg' the system to allow us to control our fertility, we are slaves. The means for this must be in our own hands."

— a quote from the book *From Housewife to Heretic*
by Sonja Johnson

Children, Parenting, and Self-Esteem

I would like to talk a little about children and parenting. I know I have had many children in my many lifetimes. This lifetime I do not have them. I accept this as perfect for me this time around. The Universe has filled my life with rich experiences and has made me a surrogate mother to millions.

Please don't buy into the belief that a woman is unfulfilled without a child. This may be true for most women, but not for all. Society insists that all women must have babies, which is a good way to keep women in their places. I always believe that there is a reason for everything. If you do not have children, then perhaps you are meant to do other things in life. If you long for children and acutely feel this as a loss, then grieve about it. And then move on. Don't sit in the grieving process forever. Affirm for yourself:

> *"I know that everything that happens in my life is for my highest good. I am deeply fulfilled."*

There are so many abandoned children in this world. If we really want to fulfill the maternal instinct, then rescue and adoption is a good alternative. We can mother other women. We can take a lost woman under our wing and help her to fly. We can rescue animals. I have four dogs and two bunny rabbits. All of these animals have been rescued from shelters. Each one comes with its own history of abuse. I have learned that a year of love can do wonders for all of us, including animals. We can work in many ways to better the world.

An enormous industry is growing up to "sell" fertility; it has become a $2 billion business, and the fertility clinics often use an aggressive hard sell. There is almost no regulation to this industry. You certainly don't want pregnancy to become an exercise in desperation while you put your life on hold. In-vitro fertilization has become a new social fad, and it is not a healthy one. If your body is meant to have a baby, then it will. If your body does not get pregnant, there is a good reason. Accept it. There are other things to do with your life. You may find a calling that could surprise you.

My personal belief is to stay away from fertility treatments. We don't know enough about these experimental treatments yet. Doctors are experimenting with women's bodies and with fetuses. Fertility treatments are very expensive, and I think they are dangerous. We are now beginning to read about some of the horrors associated with these treatments. One woman who had 40 treatments, at vast expense, did not get pregnant, but she did get aids[1]. One of the many donors she used had aids. I have read of couples who mortgage their house to pay for treatment and still have no success. Be very careful before you begin fertility treatments. Read everything you can find on the subject, not just the literature handed out by the fertility clinic. Be informed and be aware.

The subject of abortion in this culture is not an easy one, as we have so many quite violent beliefs surrounding it. It's not like China, where women are forced to have abortions to keep the population down. We have made abortion a moral, and even a political issue; the Chinese have made it a necessity. The anti-abortion groups are really saying that women must be kept in their place. We must breed, and we must serve our families. Our reproductive capacity is even being treated as a political issue. The decision to have an abortion is always a difficult one. While it would be better not to have to do it, I would never condemn a woman who finds herself in a desperate situation and makes the decision to abort.

I have heard of Indian medicine women in Northern Baja, Mexico, who say there are

[1] I always spell *aids* with lower-case letters to diminish the importance of the dis-ease.

herbs to prevent pregnancy. They are taken twice and give total birth control for eight years with no side effects. I have always known that Nature has a remedy for everything if we are only willing to learn her secrets. Those of us who are more "civilized," sophisticated, and farther away from nature turn to chemicals and surgery for our answers.

I look forward to the time when we have learned to mentally accept or reject pregnancy. I know this is one of the things we are capable of doing with our minds. We just haven't learned how yet. Scientists say we only use 10 percent of our brain. I am sure that one day we will unleash the other 90 percent and find we have powers we cannot even imagine at this time.

Bringing Up Our Children to Love Themselves

There are also many single mothers struggling to raise children alone. It is a very difficult job, and I applaud each and every woman who goes through this experience. These women really know what "tired" means. With the divorce rate as it is, a question every bride needs to ask herself before having children is: "Am I willing and able to raise my children by myself?" Raising children is more work than many brides anticipate. Raising children as a single parent is overwhelming. As a society, we must insist that adequate child care is provided for all women who work. Women must help create laws that work for women and children.

As mothers, we don't have to be "Super Women," and we don't have to be "Perfect Parents." If you want to learn new skills, read some of the great books that are now out on parenting, such as Wayne Dyer's *What Do You Really Want for Your Children?* If you are a loving parent, your children will have an excellent chance of growing up to be the sort of people you would like to have as friends. They will be people who are self-fulfilled and successful. Self-fulfillment brings inner peace. I think the best thing we can do for our children is to learn to love ourselves, for children always learn by example. You will improve the quality of your life, and so will they. The self-esteem you create for yourself will bring self-esteem to your whole family.

There is also a positive side to being a single parent. Now women have an opportunity to raise their sons to be the men they say they want. Women complain so much about the behavior and attitudes of men, and yet women raise the sons. If we want men who are kind, loving, and in touch with their feminine sides, then it is up to us to raise them that way. What is it you want in a man, in a husband? I suggest that you write these things down, and be very clear about what you *do* want. Then teach your son to be that way. His wife will love you for it, and you and your son will have a good relationship forever.

Please, if you are a single mother, do not bad-mouth your ex-husband. This only teaches your children that marriage is war, and when they grow up, their marriages will be a battlefield. A mother has more influence over the child than anyone else. Mothers unite! When women get it together, we can have the kind of men we say we want—in just one generation.

I would like to see self-esteem and self-worth taught in all the elementary schools as a daily class. Empower the young children, and we'll have empowered adults. I get letters every so often from women and men who teach school, and they tell me about the wonderful results they get when they teach these methods. It's great to see what they can do with the kids. Usually they only have the children for one grade. But even so, they can instill some positive ideas in each child.

As our daughters learn to empower themselves, they will not allow themselves to be abused or diminished in any way. And, our sons will learn to have respect for everyone, including all the women in their lives. No baby boy is born an abuser, and no baby girl is born a victim or lacking in self-worth. Abuse of others and lack of self-esteem is *learned* behavior. Children are taught violence and taught to accept victimhood. If we want the adults in our society to treat each other with respect, then we must raise our children to be gentle and to have self-respect. Only in this way will the two sexes truly honor each other.

If you are a parent, you have an opportunity to be an example. You can teach your children affirmations and mirror work. Children love to do mirror work. Work on this together in front of a mirror. You can do affirmations for each other. Help each other create positive experiences. The family that affirms together has a great life. Let your children know how important their thoughts are. Children will learn that they are partly responsible for their own experiences; they are co-creators in life—which gives them the power to make changes.

Parents have a tendency to repress many emotions. In each marriage, there is usually some unspoken/uncommunicated problems that have not been dealt with. Children pick up on this and act out these issues. What we call the terrible twos really happens when children begin to mirror their parents' repressed feelings. The teenage years are an escalation of this pattern. Parents have a tendency to blame the children rather than cleaning up their own stuff. If your child is acting up, what suppressed emotional problems of yours could they be mirroring? When you have released your resentment and forgiven your issues, then you will find that your children will miraculously change for the better.

In life, we often confuse the messenger with the message and lose the lesson. When our children, or others, do something to really bother us, we usually get angry and blame them. What we are not realizing is that these people are only playing a part in our play. They are mirroring some belief or pattern or suppressed issue *within* us. They are showing us something we are now being given an opportunity to release. Next time you get very angry at someone, try to step back and ask yourself, "What is the lesson here? How does this incident remind me of something from my childhood? What is the pattern that I'm looking for? Am I willing to forgive myself or those involved with the original incident?"

Our children and our friends often show us things about ourselves that we really don't want to look at or deal with. We do love to run from our lessons.

✴ Chapter VI ✴

Creating Your Own Good Health

We women need to keep ourselves informed about the many alternative methods of treating our bodies. We can't simply rely on the manufacturers of pills. Advertisements on television will never give us the information we need. Over-the-counter drugs may mask a symptom, but they have nothing to do with true healing. If we hold on to old belief systems about a woman's place and continue to use old methods of managing our health, we will find it difficult to be empowered.

It is time for us to take our power back from the medical and pharmaceutical industries. We have been buffeted about by high-tech medicine, which is very expensive and which often destroys our health. It is time for all of us to learn to take control of our own bodies and create good health for ourselves, thereby saving millions of lives and billions of dollars. When we really understand the body/mind connection, most of our health problems will disappear

Your local health food store is filled with publications that teach you how to keep your body healthy. Everything you learn about yourself and about life empowers you. I highly recommend the book *Women's Bodies, Women's Wisdom* by Christiane Northrup, M.D. Dr. Northrup, a renowned holistic physician, has become a mentor of mine. I also suggest that you become a member of her Health Wisdom for Women Network. She puts out a monthly publication that will keep you informed of how to heal your symptoms naturally and give you the latest updates on women's health issues.

The Importance of Our Diet

Nutrition plays an extremely important role in our health and well-being. In many ways, we are what we eat. My basic philosophy on food is: If it grows, eat it; if it does not grow, don't eat it. Fruits, vegetables, nuts, and grains grow. Twinkies and Coca-Cola do not grow. I believe that fast-food outlets are destroying the health of America. Are you aware that the five biggest-selling items in supermarkets are Coca Cola, Pepsi-Cola, Campbell's Soup, processed cheese, and beer? These items have no food value, are filled with sugar and salt, and contribute to the epidemic of dis-ease we have in this country. Learn about nutrition. It is imperative for your health. Processed foods cannot build health no matter how beautiful the picture the manufacturer has put on the package.

Women are going to live a long time, so we have much work to do make this planet a better place for all other women. We must be strong, flexible, and healthy in order to accomplish this. When you see older women who are frail, ill, and incapacitated, you are often looking at a lifetime of inadequate nutrition, lack of exercise, and an accumulation of negative thoughts and beliefs. It does not have to be that way. We women need to learn how to take care of our magnificent bodies so that we sail into our older years in perfect physical shape. I had a physical recently, and the doctor told me I was in amazingly good physical condition for someone my age. It disturbed me that he expected a woman of 70 to be in poor health!

The cells in your body are living and, as such, need living food to grow and reproduce. Fresh foods are essential to our diets. Life has already provided us with everything we need to feed ourselves and to remain healthy. The simpler we can eat, the healthier we will be. We need to pay attention to what we put in our bodies! Because if we don't, who will? We prevent dis-ease through conscious living. If an hour after lunch you feel sleepy, then something you have eaten has created an allergic reaction. Pay attention to what you eat. Look for the foods that give you great energy.

As much as possible, eat organic fruits and vegetables. I learned in Dr. Andrew Weil's *Self-Healing* monthly newsletter that the supermarket fruits and vegetables that contain the most pesticides are (in order): strawberries, bell peppers, spinach, U.S.-grown cherries, peaches, Mexican-grown cantaloupe, celery, apples, apricots, green beans, grapes from Chile, and cucumbers.

Don't listen to the dairy or meat industries. They don't care about your health; they're only interested in profits. Eating lots of red meat and dairy products is not good for women's bodies. Merely eliminating these foods from your diet can often clear up PMS problems and help alleviate menopause symptoms. Caffeine and sugar are the two other culprits that contribute to most of the problems that women have with their health. Learn to eat in a healthy manner. Your body will thank you by giving you renewed energy. Take your power back. Learn about your body. When you eat for health, you will never have to diet.

The Benefits of Exercise

One great way to increase our well-being is to exercise. Exercise is vital to our health. If we don't exercise at all, then our bones weaken; they require exercise to stay strong. We are living longer all the time, and we want to be able to run and jump and dance and move easily until our last day. Find some movement that you enjoy, and do it. Everything that you do for yourself is either an act of self-love or self-hate. Exercise is self-love, and loving yourself is the key to success in every aspect of your life.

A great "one-minute" exercise is to jump up and down 100 times. It is quick, easy, and it makes you feel good. Let yourself dance to music. Run around the block just once.

You could get yourself a little mini trampoline and bounce on that, gently at first. It is a really fun exercise, and every time you bounce, it helps clean the lymph system and strengthens the heart and the bones. The inventor of the mini trampoline is now in his 80s and is still spreading the good news of exercise and aging. Don't ever buy into the idea that you are too old for exercise.

Some Thoughts on Smoking

Stopping smoking is one of the best things you can do for your health. As a smoker, even if you are not one of the 400,000 people who die of cigarette-related diseases each year, you are still contributing to your health problems. From ovary problems to lung cancer to heart disease and osteoporosis, cigarettes increase the risks. Addiction and denial play a powerful role during pregnancy if a woman insists on smoking throughout her nine-month term. For vanity reasons alone, a woman could find a good reason to stop. Smoking enlarges pores, creates lines around the mouth, and ages the skin prematurely. It also makes a woman smell like a dirty ash-tray. If you decide to stop smoking, there is lots of help available. Your health food store has many products to rebalance your body. Acupuncture, hypnosis, and traditional Chinese medicine all help with withdrawal. Your body will love you when you respect it in return. Removing harmful substances from your body is an act of self-love.

Menopause: Natural and Normal

I believe that menopause is a normal, natural process of life. It is not meant to be a disease. Each month during menstruation, the body sloughs off the bed that was prepared for a baby that was not conceived. It also releases many toxins at that time. If we eat a junk-food diet or even the standard American diet of processed foods—20 percent sugars and 37 percent fat—we are building up toxins all the time, perhaps more than we can eliminate.

If we carry a lot of toxins in our bodies when we are on the brink of menopause, then the process will be more uncomfortable. So, the better you take care of your body on a daily basis, the easier your menopause time will be. A difficult or easy menopause period begins with how we feel about ourselves and how we take care of ourselves from puberty on. Women who are experiencing a difficult menopause are usually people who have eaten poorly for a long time and also have poor mental self-images.

In the 1900s, our life spans were about 49 years. In those days, menopause was no big deal. By the time you had menopause, you were on your way out. Today our life spans are around 80 years, and will soon go into the 90s, so menopause is an issue that must be dealt with. More and more women today are choosing to take a more active, responsible role in their health care, to grow more in harmony with their bodies, and to allow processes of change such as menopause to unfold naturally for them, with little discomfort or diminished capacities. Baby-boomer women are entering a new era, that of the "menoboomers." So of course with the aging of the baby boomers has come an intense explosion of interest in the menopausal transition of life. It is estimated that approximately 60 million American women will be entering this hormonal and physiologic landmark of reproductive life by the year 2000.

Traditional American Indian women do not experience menopause; they continue to menstruate until they die. The menstrual cycle was considered a sign of health by Indian women. The Northern Baja women today, who are about 100 years behind the times, still continue to have their menstrual cycle until old age. They do not understand the concept of menopause. The menstrual cycle was a time of wisdom, and Indian women's knowledge was sought after. In the past, it was normal for Indian women to have children in their 60s. Of course, it is less and less common now due to the fast pace of life, poor diet, and so on, in these modern times. I am sure that if we study more of the other indigenous cultures around the world, we will find more natural ways of managing the normal menstrual cycle. I have heard that one of the reasons why traditional Japanese women do not have hot flashes is because they eat so many soybean products.

Estrogen therapy scares me. Most of our information comes from the pharmaceutical companies and is biased towards selling their chemical products. I agree that it is a positive treatment for some women. However, I do not believe that "mass-scale estrogen therapy for women, from puberty to grave," as some doctors recommend, is a good idea. Premarin, which is so popular today, is made from a pregnant mare's urine. How can that possibly help a woman's body? Nature in all her wisdom has created our bodies to function perfectly till the last day, to heal themselves, and to live a long time. We must trust this knowledge, as well as our inner wisdom, rather than listen to groups who want us to believe that our bodies will deteriorate with dis-ease after menopause.

I would like to see studies done on healthy women who just sail through menopause without any problems. When I went through menopause, I only had one hot flash. I was given a homeopathic remedy, and that was the end of my hot flash.

We are learning that progesterone is often more beneficial to us than estrogen. Many times when we think we have an estrogen deficiency, we really have a progesterone deficiency. Natural progesterone, which comes from wild Mexican yams, also stimulates bone formation. It encourages the osteoblast cells to lay down new bone. Remember: Bone is a living tissue, and bone loss can be reversed. Natural progesterone can be purchased from health food stores in the form of a cream. This cream is applied to the soft inner tissue of the body where it is well absorbed. It has none of the side effects of synthetic estrogen. It is also beneficial for alleviating PMS and many menopause symptoms.

I am not suggesting that there are not some women who are helped by hormone replacement therapy (HRT). However, for many in the medical establishment to now make the statement that *all* women need HRT from menopause until death is to condemn and belittle the midlife woman. Essentially, what I am suggesting is that striving for harmony and balance in our bodies and our minds can make potentially debilitating side-effect-ridden drug therapies unnecessary.

As with everything else in our lives, we all

experience different degrees of readiness and willingness. For many of us, the level of responsibility and commitment necessary to bring our minds and bodies into harmony when it comes to deep-seated issues is too great. We need help from the medical profession or other sources until we feel ready or safe enough to confront some of the issues impacting our health, such as beliefs about self-worth. A far too common belief, in our patriarchal society, is that women have little or no worth without their reproductive powers. Is it any wonder that many women fear and resist menopause? Estrogen therapy does not address these types of issues. Only our hearts and minds can heal these perceptions.

I repeat: Menopause is not a dis-ease. It is a normal, natural process of life. However, marketing menopause is becoming a big business, and almost all of our information is coming from the pharmaceutical companies. It is imperative that we women educate ourselves about what our real choices are. Please read and share with your friends the book, *The Menopause Industry: How the Medical Establishment Exploits Women,* by Sandra Coney. This book points out that until the

1960s, doctors were not very interested in menopause. Women were told that it was all in their heads. It also states: "There is no area that demonstrates the entrenched sexism of medicine more sharply than that of menopause. The new view of menopause as dis-ease is socially controlling. Modern medicine does not make women more powerful and in control of their lives. It makes patients out of well women."

There are many herbs used by nutritionists and many homeopathic remedies that are very helpful when you are going through this time of life. There are also natural substances that take the place of estrogen. Speak to your nutritionist about these matters. Remember, women today are pioneers who are working to change old, negative belief patterns so that our daughters and our daughters' daughters will never have to suffer during menopause. We can learn to plan for our menopause the way we now can plan for our pregnancies.

In your daily meditation, be sure to send love to every part of your body, especially your whole genital/reproductive area. Thank these organs for serving you so well. Tell them you will do everything you can to keep them healthy. Develop a loving relationship with this part of your body. Honoring your body will strengthen these organs. Ask your uterus or ovaries what they want from you. Together, plan your menopause as a simple transition time—comfortable for your organs and comfortable for your emotions. Love heals, and loving your body helps create well-beingness.

Cosmetic Surgery: Doing It for the Right Reasons

There's nothing wrong with cosmetic surgery as long as the reasons for it are valid. We need to be very clear that cosmetic surgery will not cure emotional problems, will not dissolve self-hatred, nor will it save a marriage. Too often we have cosmetic surgery because we feel we're not good enough. We will never feel good enough if we only have surgery. Surgery does not cure beliefs. When I look at the proliferation of cosmetic surgery advertising, I see an industry that feeds off women's lack of self-worth.

I've seen women who have a lot of self-hatred get cosmetic surgery because they thought it would make them beautiful. Due to their self-loathing, they picked the wrong surgeon, so now they look worse than before the operation. I remember one very pretty girl who had no self-worth, no self-love. She felt that if only her nose were different she would be okay. She insisted on surgery for the wrong reasons, and now she has a nose that looks like a pig's. Her problem had nothing to do with her nose.

You cannot use cosmetic surgery to improve your self-worth. It will never happen. You might have a temporary improvement. Soon the old feelings of unworthiness will come up, and you'll start thinking, Well, maybe if I have this other wrinkle removed... and the process never ends. Somebody told me the other day about elbow surgery that can help you when your elbows get baggy as you age. I said to myself, "Oh, my goodness, how far can we go? Wouldn't it be easier to wear slightly longer sleeves?" But again, the media has programmed us so much. According to commercial advertisers, we must all be perfect little anorectic teenage girls with no wrinkles and no flesh. However, we can't place *all* the blame on the advertisers—*we're* the ones who buy their products. I think when women develop more self-worth and self-esteem, they won't care what the magazines say, and the ads will change.

Don't let doctors experiment with your body. When we use unnatural methods to force the body to do something or have something that in its wisdom it does not want to do or have, we are asking for trouble. Don't fool around with Mother Nature. Look at all the problems many women are having because of breast implants. If your breasts are small, rejoice in them. Sending love to your breasts combined with positive affirmations has increased bust sizes for some women. It is a good way to love your body, and your body loves to be loved. I also believe that your body is exactly what you chose to have when you decided to incarnate this time. Be happy with who you are. Above all, don't alter your body to please someone else. If people don't love you as you are, they will not love you any more after you sacrifice your body for them.

So, if you do decide to have a little nip and tuck, be very clear as to *why* you are doing it. Put a lot of love into your body before, during, and after surgery. I would say affirmations something like this:

I have a loving surgeon who does beautiful work. The procedure is quick and easy, and everything goes perfectly. The doctor is delighted with how quickly I heal. I am very pleased with the results. All is well, and I am safe.

Breast Cancer: What Does It Represent?

There is a consistent pattern that I've noticed with almost every woman who has breast cancer. These women usually have a tremendous inability to say no. Breasts represent nourishment, and people with breast cancer seem to nourish everybody in their world except themselves. They find it very difficult to say no. They often were raised by parents who used guilt and manipulation for discipline. Now they are adult people-pleasers surrounded by people who are constantly asking them to do more than they can comfortably do. These women keep straining themselves for others and saying yes to demands that they really don't want to do. They give and give until there is no nourishment left for them.

Learning to say no can be very difficult at first because the people around you that have been interacting with you have become used to you saying yes. And when you first say no, they get angry. You can expect that reaction. Anybody who is learning to say no has to put up with anger for a while. The first time you say no is the hardest. When you learn to say no, it is very important that you do not make excuses, because the minute you do so, they've got you. The other person can always talk you out of your excuse. Just say a simple no. "No, I can't do that." "Not anymore." "No, I don't do that anymore." Any short statement that sends a definite "no" message will do the trick. The other person will obviously get angry, and then you have to know that their anger has nothing to do with *you*. It has to do with *them*. Just remember to say to yourself: WHEN I SAY NO TO YOU, I AM SAYING YES TO ME. Repeat this powerful affirmation to yourself, and it will make you feel good. By the time you've said no three times to the other person, he or she will stop asking you, realizing that you have become a different person. You are coming from a different place inside.

It can be very difficult for people-pleasers to say the first no. I remember that I was sweating the first time I stood up for myself. I thought my world would end and that I would lose out. My world did not end; it changed, and I had more self-respect. So, realize that this is just a process you are going to have to go through. Other people get angry because you are not giving, or over giving, and they might even call you selfish. But what they are really saying is that you are not doing what *they* want you to do. That's all it means. Remember that when you say no to them, you are saying yes to yourself. You are dissolving your internal resentment at the same time.

I know somebody who has just recently left her husband for a period of time; it may not be a permanent situation. Now her husband has nobody to blame for the things that go wrong. It can't be his wife's fault—she's not even there. He is learning to look at life in a different way. Her two adult sons are now respecting her because she has stood up for herself, and she is doing what she wants to do for a change. It's very interesting to watch the whole family change. It was difficult for her to make the move, but she did it, and her whole life has turned around. There comes a time for every woman when she needs to ask herself, "What is it that's best for *me?*" This may be a new question for women to ask. Ann Landers tells women who are contemplating separation or divorce to ask themselves, "Would I be better off if I left or if I stayed?"

We Need to Take Care of Our Hearts

While 4 percent of women succumb to breast cancer, 36 percent of women will die of heart disease. We hear so much about the dangers of breast cancer but little about women and the risks of heart disease. Yet, heart disease is a leading cause of death for women. Women are also more likely to die of complications from coronary bypass surgery than are men.

Taking care of our hearts is very important for women. A high-fat diet is not good for any of us. On the physical level, a high-fat diet, lack of exercise, and smoking all contribute to cardiovascular disease. These are things we can do something about. Our hearts never attack us; we attack our hearts.

On the emotional level, the heart, and the

blood it pumps, represents love and joy and our early connections to family. Women with heart problems usually have unresolved family issues that take the joy and the love out of their lives. These issues might keep love and joy from entering their lives because they are afraid to let love in. Closing our heart to love is very symbolic of shutting off the flow of life to our heart.

The emotional cause for so many diseases keeps coming back to the issue of forgiveness. The spiritual lesson of forgiveness is a difficult one for all of us. Yet it is one that everyone has to learn if we want to have true healing. We each experience betrayal or loss or abuse of some form. Forgiving the experience and those involved is part of spiritual maturity. It is over and done and cannot be changed. Letting it go frees us from bondage to the past. It is the act of releasing the past that frees us to live in the now. We cannot be happy and healthy and prosperous and free as long as we are stuck in the past and we won't forgive. Those are the biggest issues we have, all of us, and it's our biggest spiritual lesson to forgive, to love ourselves, and to live in the now. This heals the heart.

Once a day, sit quietly and place your hands upon your heart. Send it love, and allow yourself to feel the love your heart has for you. It has been beating for you since before you were born and will work for you as long as you choose to live. Look into your heart and see if there is any bitterness or resentment lingering there. Gently wash it away with forgiveness and understanding. If you could but just see the larger picture, you would understand the lessons. Send love to each member of your family and forgive them. Feel your heart relaxing and being at peace. Your heart is love, and the blood in your veins is joy. Your heart is now lovingly pumping joy throughout your body. All is well, and you are safe.

✷ Chapter VII ✷

Exploring Sexuality

I'd like to briefly discuss a few of my ideas on sexuality, unpopular though they may be, and some of the changes that are going on. We may need to adjust our thinking in this area, too. We as a society have so many condemning beliefs about our sexuality. Remember: No matter what your sexual orientation is, it is perfect for you. When we are referring to relationships, it applies to all of us, no matter if your relationship is heterosexual or homosexual. Even science is now recognizing that sexual orientation is something that we are born with and not something that we choose. If you are heterosexual, imagine what it would feel like if you were told you had to become a lesbian.

It would be almost impossible. It is the same when you ask a lesbian to become heterosexual. I feel that we need to apologize to our lesbian sisters for the appalling ways we have denounced them. It is tribal outcasting at its worst level. We must not put ourselves or anyone else down for something as simple and natural as sexuality. This particular social prejudice keeps us from participating in the larger picture of Life. Love yourself as you are. God has never made a mistake.

Today we are finding that many older women, who would never have thought of doing so in the past, are now beginning to explore a gay lifestyle and turning to other women for intimate relationships. With the scarcity of men in this age group, it makes perfect sense. Why would we choose to be alone when love is waiting for us? Intimacy with another woman can reveal depths that women have never experienced before. Women in relationships can be more loving and caring than many men allow themselves to be. Also, other women are usually more accepting and understanding of bodily changes that happen as we get older.

Many of you may be unaware that in

Victorian days, the prevalence of separate worlds (in business, politics, parenting, etc.) for men and women made male-female relations extremely strained, so women commonly turned to other women for their most intimate relationships. A woman's diary might go on for pages about a female friend and then state briefly, "I accepted the marriage proposal of Mr. S. last night." Romantic friendships were also common among young middle-class men. No one considered such relationships a sign of homosexuality. In fact, the term wasn't even invented until the late 19th century. This was also a time when prostitution was in its prime: New York City had one prostitute for every 64 men, and Savannah, Georgia, had a 1-to-39 ratio.

So, my point is: Love is where we find it. Fashions in love change from country to country and century to century. We have certain so-called norms at the moment, but they too will change in time. Realize that we do have options in sexuality if we choose to take them. As long as we come from a loving heart and only want the best for everyone around us, we want to be free to make our own choices. Some of us will even choose to be asexual, and that is okay, too. Let's drop the judgments and rejoice in love when we see it. When we are giving and receiving love, we are nurturing our souls and emanating good energy.

✳ ✳ ✳

✵ Chapter VIII ✵

Sexual Harassment and Speaking Out

How many times have you been dishonored or sexually assaulted and said ***nothing?*** How many times have you blamed yourself when a man has been out of line? "Oh, maybe it was my fault. Maybe I just imagined it. Oh, well, it goes with the territory. This wasn't as bad as some things I've encountered."

There is not a woman reading this book who has not been verbally abused; or grabbed, pinched, or fondled by someone who had no business touching us. And yet, most of us keep quiet; we say nothing. It's time that we learn to speak out and stand up for ourselves. If we don't, we will never stop this nonsense.

I had an incident recently in my own home involving a couple who worked for me—a marvelous English couple who took such good care of me and my home and my animals for almost four years. It all started out so well, but over time, little things occurred, mainly with him. They were such small things, though, that at the time I let them go. Big mistake. He became increasingly lazy and let his wife do two-thirds of the work. He began to forget that I was the employer and started to act as if the house was his. He became too familiar—like he was one of my friends. All of this slowly crept up until it developed into inappropriate behavior. I see now that I did not read the signals correctly, and I didn't keep up the appropriate boundaries. I realize that I got to a point where I was not honoring the little feelings that say that something is not right. I was beginning to walk on eggshells so that I wouldn't disturb *him*—to keep *him* in a good mood.

The day after my 70th birthday party, which was a marvelous affair, I discovered that he was groping and grabbing many of my women friends. When I talked with some of them, I found out that this had been going on for over a year at various functions. *But no one had told me.* Once the veil was lifted, a floodgate of information poured in to me. He had been hitting on several of my employees, even molesting some of them. My personal secretary had been attacked in my own home while I was out of town. I was horrified. This was happening to Louise Hay's friends and employees! But why didn't they tell me? They were frightened; they were embarrassed—they all had different reasons. You probably know what some of them are, because you may have used them yourself. I thought back to all the times in the past I'd put up with various forms of sexual abuse and how I usually just wanted to escape from the situation and have it over with. But how many times had I actually spoken up or blown the whistle?

I also came to discover that this man abused his wife and that she often carried bruises. I thought, Look at the secrets we keep; look how we let men get away with violating our space and our honor. Fear beats us into submission on every level. A great heaviness came over my heart as I listened to these tales. And perhaps it was only the tip of the iceberg. To all those women who were at my 70th birthday party, I apologize for any inappropriate behavior that may have occurred.

One of my very close friends who always shares so much with me—and who considers herself an enlightened woman with a lot of self-esteem—didn't even speak up. When dealing with an abuse issue, her first reaction was to remain silent and not make waves.

In any case, while things had not *felt* right at home for some time, now I had something to deal with, for this man had really gone too far. I assembled a support team, because there was no way that I would have confronted him and his wife by myself. Even so, if I had not trusted my information so much, I could have easily been taken in by his excellent performance of total denial. When he realized I wasn't buying his story, he turned vicious and nasty. However, I not only had my support team, I also had the phone in my hand, thinking that 911 was easy to punch in. I said that I wanted him out of the house and off the property by morning. My palms were sweating, there was a knot in my stomach—*and* I felt a sense of power. It wasn't easy for me to stand up to a big 6'5" man who was very angry. While I had a lot of compassion for his wife, I also know that she was an enabler, and the only way she could handle his womanizing was to be in total denial, or to blame those he fondled. Often when a husband is a womanizer, an abuser, the wife will keep herself in denial by making the other women wrong. So they both came off as the innocent and injured parties. They were also packed and out of the house in three-and-a-half hours.

My girlfriend called me the next day, incredulous, telling me that she had actually started to wonder: "Could I have imagined it? Could I have been mistaken? Did I cost a man his job by speaking up?" We women have such a tendency to *let it go,* don't we? Who are we—just "girls," after all—to say anything? Sure, maybe we imagined it. We often believe the denial by the man. Our space and honor have been called into question, and yet it's our word that's doubted. The old tapes in our psyche cause us to further disempower the woman. So much denial goes on. Women have been controlled by terror for eons. We have allowed this to happen for so many lifetimes out of fear, usually justified. In the past, it could have meant our lives if we'd spoken up. Even today, in Afghanistan, the current government has just reinstated stoning for adultery. But of course it means stoning of the woman—never the man.

The minute I clearly saw what was happening in my home, I took appropriate action to end the situation. I also called a good therapist and made an appointment. Even though I've done much therapy in the past, I was very aware that there must still be a part of me that attracts this behavior—not violence to my own being, but in my own household. I will do whatever it takes to clear the rest of the pattern within me.

My therapist asked me about my anger as a child toward my abusive stepfather. "I cannot remember any anger, only fear," I told her.

She asked, "Well, wasn't there a time when you got angry and sassed him back?" I knew immediately that she had never been an abused child. I was beaten daily for being the best little girl I could be; what on earth would have happened to me if I had been bad enough to sass him? No, I don't remember anger; I only remember fear and terror.

When we are beaten into submission often enough, we lose all hope of ever making things different. Then we grow up into women who are still governed by the reactions of the little girl inside of us. This can happen in the best of homes. Dishonoring little girls is far too widespread. We need to teach girls when they are very young—in elementary school and perhaps even younger—that they need to *speak up* when someone abuses them in some way. If we are to make this world a safe place for women everywhere, we must change our reactions, even when it seems to be very difficult. Firing that man was my way of standing up to my stepfather—something I could have never done as a child.

✳ ✳ ✳

I have created so much harmony in my workplace. Everyone talks about how great it is to do business with Hay House. I have happy employees. An ex-union organizer said to me recently that he had never seen a warehouse crew that was so happy. Yet, in my own home, I allowed a disempowering, abusive situation to develop because I did not read the signals, and for one reason or another, I did not want to make waves.

In a way, it is a blessing that this situation occurred, because now I will speak out *for* all women and *to* all women. I will speak up, because if I don't, how can I expect other women to be vocal? We see men as authority figures, and we see ourselves as the victims. That's how we've been brought up—to think that we couldn't win even if we tried. There are so many insidious ways of discounting, dishonoring, and disempowering women. We've fought for our self-worth, and still we find it difficult or impossible to speak out. The training that submissive women have had is so strong that we must learn to be vigilant about the slightest encroachment of our boundaries. We've been taught to shift and to carry a man's load for him—first our fathers, then our boyfriends, bosses, and husbands. We have done this for so long that we think it's normal. We must learn to blow the whistle. It is the fear of embarrassment and violence that keeps us silent. How many women live in the atmosphere of a battlefield, and how many children are raised in this environment? How do women stop this? By knowing we can. By refusing to be silent. Women have allowed it, and it is up to women to stop it. It could not have gone on for this long without the permission of women, stated or unstated. We must stop allowing it to continue.

If we are willing to be vigilant in saying no, we can get in the *habit* of saying no. Then we can turn the whole situation of abuse around. Being silent is a detriment to us as women and to our whole society. It has now been 25 years since the birth of the women's liberation movement, and this behavior—verbal abuse and sexual violation—is still so prevalent. It seems to be par for the course at most offices and workplaces. It is what women have had to put up with. So it's time for us to stop allowing ourselves to be abused by ourselves, or by the people around us. Let's tell the truth; let's tell the secrets. Opening up will stop the behavior. If men can't get away with it, they will stop doing it. Don't collude with men—it dishonors ourselves, and it dishonors *all* women. Today we no longer have to accept abuse of any sort if we will just stand up and speak up. Each one of us who speaks out creates the space for others to tell the truth.

We must learn to put up the appropriate boundaries that honor us. What are these boundaries that women need to put up to ensure that we are always honored? First, we have to come from a place where we believe that we *deserve* boundaries. We often do not pick up on the signals of danger, that something is not right. Then it comes as a shock and a violation when something happens. Abuse is a power play. It controls and manipulates us. We keep silent because we fear losing the job; we fear the repercussions that might ensue. We even keep silent when we are about to make love to a man who is not wearing a condom. We *want* to speak up and shout, "I respect myself, and I will not allow you to endanger me. Put on a condom or leave!" But do we? Not often enough—due to fear, embarrassment, and shame.

When we keep silent, like the silence of the lambs, we are led to slaughter. We become too embarrassed to speak up. We remember the reactions we got when we *did*. They laughed at us; they thought it was a joke. They discounted us or made us feel as though *we* were troublemakers. So it becomes the rule that we don't share and don't tell. Keep peace; don't make waves. This is how abuse is allowed to continue.

We women must balance the scales of power. Violence and sexual abuse—they are the two areas where women are most vulnerable. We must learn to treat all incidents with a no-nonsense attitude—to be very matter-of-fact, businesslike instead of vulnerable. We do not have to be angry bitches who yell at every man, but we do need to be women who come from love and compassion and yet operate with iron-glove firmness.

We must build up our self-worth so that we *will* say no. We must open our eyes and our intuition to the insidious ways in which things creep up. Tell the story from the beginning. Call them on the little things. Refuse to tolerate poor behavior. Reach out for help. Put a stop to it at once. Men see what they can get away with, and then they push just a little bit more—or a lot more. We must begin to stop any abusive behavior at the onset when it is so small that it's hard to say something. What is the first sign of abuse? Call the man on it immediately. Also, be prepared that he will meet it with denial. Men have used that cover for so long. "Who me? I would never do that! I have never done that in my life!" Some men are so fast, so smooth, so practiced, so professional. When we accept their excuses, then the woman conspires with the man. Women become the enablers. We become part of the destructive force of society whenever we go along with the secret. So we really need to look at the secrets we keep. Women have been walking on eggshells, accommodating the abusers, being the nurturing ones. It's time for us to begin nurturing *ourselves.*

I don't have all the answers, but I do have a big mouth. I will speak up on this issue whenever I talk in public. I will encourage women everywhere to educate themselves on these issues—to speak up, to stand up, to be troublemakers if we have to. Collectively, we can heal this issue in one generation. We can save our daughters from what we've had to go through.

We need to begin teaching classes for women on how to honor ourselves. We need to develop ways to prepare ourselves so that we have options when we find ourselves violated or about to be violated. It will be like learning a fire-alarm drill—to be prepared and empowered at all times. Developing self-worth, self-love, and self-esteem is essential, or we won't believe that we deserve to be honored and protected.

Let's learn to put up an energy barrier—a mental power shield that makes us feel protected. One way is to visualize ourselves being empowered in every situation—at home, at work, during social occasions—everywhere. Look at the areas in your life where you don't honor or empower yourself. Make a vow to stop that. Begin to create empowerment in your mind. Visualize how you would like to be treated in each situation. Do affirmations for empowerment. This will begin the healing process, and as we heal, we will automatically teach our daughters.

By reading books and educating ourselves, we can learn that we have different options, rather than just "going along." Take the time to rehearse how you would like to take command in every situation that could possibly dishonor you. When we have a very well thought-out, well-planned course of action, then we are *empowered.* It is vital that we develop and truly understand our own self-worth, and realize that we don't have to go along with anything that doesn't feel right.

We need to teach those around us how to treat us—to say no when we feel we're about to be dishonored. "You must respect us if you wish to continue to be around us," we need to tell men. They must learn that being friendly is not a sexual invitation. When bridegrooms sleep with the bride's girlfriend or sister the night before the wedding, it is an act that dishonors us all. It is only a power play, violating the commitment, being king of the mountain.

Women must stop being enthralled with womanizers. Let's get smart. Womanizers are predators of women; they dishonor women. No matter how rich or how handsome they are, they betray us. Women often say, "Oh, he is so cute." That is no excuse for disempowering behavior. We must stop having our heads turned by ladies' men; they are just womanizers. We often reward them with admiration, and still they take away our honor. We want to honor the good character traits in men, not the ones that denigrate us. The man who seems so exciting will probably not be there to take care of the kids if we have them.

Anger toward women so often comes from mother stuff. Please don't have a relationship with, or marry, a man who hates his mother, because in time he will take it out on you. If he is willing to go to therapy, then the pattern could change; if not, he will hate women forever. As long as women are silent, we allow abuse to continue. This becomes a violation to the self, the family, the workplace, and to society, undermining the strength of our world and our future.

Do read Jennifer Coburn's book, *Take Your Power Back: A Working Woman's Response to Sexual Harassment;* also, *Too Good to Leave, Too Bad to Stay: A Step-by-Step Guide to Help You Decide Whether to Stay in or Get out of Your Relationship,* by Mira Kirshenbaum. Both are powerful books that will give you many tools for self-empowerment.

As I've said before, I have great compassion for men and the burdens they carry. But that does not mean that I will tolerate abuse. I will also never remain silent on this issue again. This is the least I can do for women!

✳ ✳ ✳

Affirmations for Honoring Ourselves

I am a valued human being.

I am always treated with respect.

I am empowered.

I am supportive of other women.

I easily speak up for myself.

I deserve to have boundaries.

My boundaries are respected.

I make waves whenever I need to.

I have a good support team.

I have integrity.

The more open I am, the safer I am.

My self-worth is very strong.

I am a woman healing other women.

I have a strong energy barrier.

The men in my life honor women.

I take my power back.

I love and honor myself.

✷ Chapter IX ✷

Getting Older: Improving the Quality of Your Life

Enough of the inordinate emphasis on the youth culture! It's time for us to help older women become all that they can be and to truly find a place of honor in this world. I want to help see that all women will experience self-love, self-worth, self-esteem, and a powerful place in society as they grow older. This is not to diminish the younger generation at all, but to truly have "equality" between the generations in the most positive way.

As I look around at our current crop of older women, I see so much fear, poor health, poverty, loneliness, and a feeling of resignation about "going downhill." I know it doesn't have to be this way. The way we currently age has been programmed into us, and we have accepted it. As a society, with some exceptions, we have come to believe that we all get old, sick, senile, frail, and die, in that order. This does not have to be the truth for us anymore. Yes, we will all die in time, but the sick, senile, and frail part is an option we do not have to experience.

It is time that we no longer accept these fears. This is a time for all of us to reverse the negative parts of aging. I believe that the second half of our lives can be even more wonderful than the first half. If we are willing to change our thinking and accept new beliefs, we can make these years our "treasure years." If we want to age successfully, then we must make a conscious choice to do so. We want more than just an increase in our longevity. We want to look forward to rich and full years ahead of us. The added years are a blank slate; what we write on them will make all the difference.

History shows us that we used to live very short lives, first only until our mid-teens, then our 30s, and then into our 40s. Even at the turn of this century, it was considered old to be 50. In 1900 our life expectancy was 47 years. Now we are accepting 80 as a normal life span. Why can't we take a quantum leap in consciousness and make the new level of acceptance 120 or 150 years?

It is not out of our reach. I see living much longer becoming normal and natural for most of us in a generation or two. I believe 75 will become the new middle age. A few years ago, a study was done at a university about aging. The researchers discovered that at whatever age you believe is middle age, that is the time your body will begin the aging process. You see, the body accepts what the mind decides upon. So, instead of accepting 45 or 50 as middle age, we could easily decide that it is now 75. The body will willingly accept that belief, too. We can reframe how we see the different stages of life.

The Center for Demographic Studies in Durham, North Carolina, has concluded that if aging patterns continue as they have since 1960, theoretical life limits could extend beyond 130 years. As recently as 1960, there were only about 3,500 centenarians. In 1995, there were about 54,000. They are the fastest-growing age group. The study found that there is no evidence of some specific age past which no human could live. They also believe that the oldest people will most likely be women.

For generations, we have allowed the numbers that correspond to how many years we have been on the planet to tell us how to feel and how to behave. As with any other aspect of life, what we mentally accept and believe about aging becomes true for us. Well, it is time for us to change our beliefs. I know that by accepting new concepts, we can make the aging process a positive, vibrant, healthy experience.

I am now in my 70th year, and I am a big, strong, healthy girl. In many ways, I feel younger than I did at 30 or 40 because I no longer feel the pressures to conform to certain standards of society. I am free to do what I want. I have stopped searching for approval, and I no longer care what anyone says about me. I walk taller, since I don't have to carry those burdens, and I find that I please myself much more often. Peer pressure has definitely become less important. In other words, for the first time in my life, I am putting myself first. And it feels good!

When I speak of living much longer lives, many women feel, "Oh, I don't want to be sick and poor for all those years." Isn't it amazing that when we open the door to new ideas and new possibilities, our minds immediately want to go into limitation thinking! We do not have to equate our later years with poverty, sickness, loneliness, and hospital deaths. If that is what we often see around us now, it is because that is what we have created due to our past belief systems. What we choose to think and believe today will create our tomorrows. We can always change our belief systems. We once believed the world was flat. Now that is no longer a truth for us.

As I said before, life comes in waves and learning experiences and periods of evolution. We are in a new period of evolution now. The Baby Boomers, those born between 1946 and 1964, were at the forefront of this dramatic shift in consciousness. People who are 50 today are approaching their later years in better shape than ever before. Our current president, Bill Clinton, who just turned 50, looks like a young man. The majority of Boomers today can easily live into their 90s.

It's almost as though we are getting two adulthoods. And we are now finding that there may be no limits to how long we can live—it is totally up to us, and how quickly we can grasp and accept new ideas about aging.

I agree that as we all live longer lives we will have to totally revamp the ways we currently structure our society, our retirement issues, our insurance, and our health care. But it can be done. Yes, this is a period of vast change for all of us. We cannot continue to live as we have in the past and still expect our lives to improve. New thinking, new ideas, and new ways of doing things are in order now.

Even our current form of housing has gotten out of touch with human qualities and closeness. I believe we also need different architecture and ways of living. Condos and retirement villages with all their rules and regulations cut elders off from life. Where are the children and grandchildren? Where is the joy and laughter? I think we need more community living. We need more duplexes—two related families living separate lives, but side by side. We could use lots of fourplexes—two families living upstairs and renting out the two lower apartments for income.

This would help to bring the elders and the children together. The children keep the elders young, and the elders give wisdom and meaning to the children's lives. It would benefit society to go back to large family living with several generations living together or nearby.

In the last couple of years, because of my "age," I've been receiving mail inviting me to live in various retirement communities and "Homes for Active Seniors." One of the enticements that always seems to be included in these offers is that a medical center is either attached or nearby. They use phrases such as "adjoining skilled nursing care facility," "all the advantages of Assisted Living Services," "24-hour Emergency Medical Services," and "supervision of medications." They are, in effect, saying, "WHEN you become ill, we will be there for you." I believe this way of thinking contributes to programming older people into believing that they WILL become sick.

I would like to see someone build a retirement community that includes a holistic health center. Instead of traditional nurses and doctors, you would find chiropractic, acupuncture, homeopathy, traditional Chinese medicine, nutrition and herbology, massage, yoga, a health club, and so on. This would be a place where everyone could look forward to healthy, carefree later years. I am sure that such a facility would have a waiting list in no time. These are the retirement homes I would like to see in the future.

The youth-worshiping culture we have created has added to the discomfort with which we regard our bodies, not to mention our fear of wrinkles. We see every change in our face and body as something to be disdained. What a terrible way to choose to feel about ourselves. Yet, it is only a thought, and a thought can be changed. The way we choose to perceive our bodies and ourselves is a learned concept. I would like to see everyone reject these false ideas and begin to love and treasure their magnificent selves, inside and out.

The young girl who does not feel good about herself will often search for reasons to hate her body, believing that there is where the fault lies. Due to the intense pressure placed upon us by the advertising world, we often believe that there is something wrong with our bodies. If only we could be thin enough, blonde enough, tall enough—if our noses were bigger or smaller, if we had a more dazzling smile—the list goes on and on. So, while we were all young at one point, few of us have ever measured up to the current standards of beauty.

As we get older, we continue to carry these feelings of inferiority with us. We find many ways, as author Doreen Virtue says, "to compare *our* insides with *their* outsides." That is, we compare how we feel inside with how other people look on the outside. These internalized feelings of not being good enough will never be healed by clothing or makeup or other superficial things. Working with affirmations to change our conscious and unconscious negative thoughts into self-loving statements such as: "I am beautiful just the way I am" and "I love the way I look" will help us make permanent changes.

It is crucial to our own well-being to constantly love and appreciate ourselves. If there is some part of your body that you are not happy with, then take a month and continually put love into that area. Literally tell your body that you love it. You might even apologize for having hated it in the past. This exercise may sound simplistic, but it works. Loving our bodies is important at any stage of our lives, and it is vital as we grow older.

Carol Hansen, in her inspirational audiocassette, *Lighten Up*, asks women to take five minutes a day to massage their bodies with lotion, telling each part you love it and thanking it for serving you. Dr. Deepak Chopra (the author of *Ageless Body, Timeless Mind*) suggests massaging your body from head to toe with sesame oil just before a shower. Any person, place, or thing that is loved will respond by being its best. The love you create for yourself now will stay with you for the rest of your life. Just as we learned to hate ourselves, so too can we learn to love ourselves. It only takes willingness and a bit of practice.

Sometimes in order to bring in new thoughts and new ideas, we first need to clean out all the old negative thoughts in our minds, just as we periodically need to clean out all the old junk in our lives. Many elders have a "depression" attitude—hoarding and storing things they no longer need. If you have stuff around your house that no longer serves you, clean these things out.

Give to the homeless or those who really need them. Have garage sales. Clean out your life and give yourself a fresh start—away from the old junk and memories of the past. Move out into life.

Your Future Is Always Bright

Just because the years are passing does not mean that the quality of our lives must automatically go downhill. I choose to see my life moving in different directions, all of them equally good. Some things are even better now than the way they were in my youth. My younger years were filled with fear; my todays are filled with confidence.

I truly believe that many of the fears we have are unnecessary. It is something we have been taught. It has been programmed into us. It is just a habitual thinking pattern, and it can be changed. Negative thinking is prevalent among so many women in their later years and, as a result, they live out their lives in discontent.

I want to help you create a conscious ideal of your later years, to help you realize that these can be the most rewarding years of your life. Know that your future is always bright, no matter what your age. See your later years becoming your treasure years. You can become an *Elder of Excellence*, someone who knows that you can be a strong, active, vital part of society no matter what your age.

As you sit quietly, bring your attention inward. Think of all the times you were joyful, and let your body feel this joy. Remember all the times you were a winner, the times when you did something you were proud of, even small things. Hold these feelings close to you, this joy and confidence. Now look forward ten years. What do you see yourself doing and being? How do you look? How do you feel? Are you carrying the joy with you? Now go 20 years down the road. What do you see? Are you alive, alert, and interested in life? Are you surrounded by friends who love you? Are you doing things that fulfill you? What is the contribution you are making to life? Right now is the time for you to visualize and create your future. Make it as healthy and as bright and joyful as you can. It is your life, and you are going to live it.

Don't ever think it is too late for you or that you are too old to dream and have goals. Dreams and goals keep us young and interested in life. Live today to the fullest, and forget about the past.

My own life really did not begin to have meaning until I was in my mid-40s. At the age of 50, I began my publishing company on a very small scale. The first year I made a profit of $42. At 55, I ventured into the world of computers. They scared me, but I took classes and overcame the fear. Today I have three computers and always travel with my lap-top At 60, I had my first garden. At this same time, I enrolled in a children's art class and began to paint. Now at 70, with each passing year, I am more creative and my life gets richer and fuller. I write, I lecture, I teach. I am constantly reading and studying. I own a very successful publishing company. I am a dedicated organic gardener. I grow most of my own food. I love people and parties. I have many loving friends. I travel extensively. I also go to an art class once a week. My life has really become a treasure chest of experiences.

Many of you, like myself, are now moving into the ranks of the elders, and it is time to view life in a different way. You don't have to live your later years the way that your parents did. You and I can create a new way of living.

We can change all the rules. When we move forward into our future, knowing and using the treasures within, then only good lies before us. We can know and affirm that everything that happens to us is for our highest good and greatest joy, truly believing that we can't go wrong.

Instead of just getting old and giving up and dying, let's learn to make a huge contribution to life. We have the time, we have the knowledge, and we have the wisdom to move out into the world with love and power. Society is facing many challenges at this time. There are many issues and problems of a global nature that require our attention. Let's look and see where we can put our energies in order to help the planet. There must be a reason that we are living longer. What are we meant to do with this extra time? If we only play "games," it gets boring after a while.

If you or a relative or a friend frequent a senior center, instead of talking about your dis-eases, talk about how you can band together and improve your corner of society. What can you do to make life better for everyone? No matter how small your contribution, it has meaning. If all elders contribute something, we can improve our country.

By activating ourselves in all segments of society, we will see our wisdom trickling down to all levels, thereby transforming our country into a place of loving kindness. So, I urge you: Step forward, use your voice, get out in the world, and LIVE! There is an opportunity for you to regain your power and create a legacy that you will be proud to pass on to your grandchildren and to their grandchildren.

Children at school are always asked, "What do you want to do when you grow up?" They are taught to plan for their future. We need to take the same attitude and plan for our later years. What do we want to be when we grow older? I want to be an Elder of Excellence, contributing to society in every way I can. Maggie Kuhn, head of the activist group The Gray Panthers, used to say, "I want to die in an airport, briefcase in hand, just finishing a job well done."

Whether we are 14, 40, or 80, we are all in the process of aging and moving toward the time when we leave the planet. Everything we do, say, and think is preparing us for the next step. Let us age with awareness and let us die with awareness. A good question for us all to ask ourselves is: "How do I want to age?" Look around you. Notice the women who are aging miserably, and notice the women who are aging magnificently. What do these two groups of women do differently? Are you willing to make the effort to be healthy, happy, and fulfilled in your later years?

The next question, then, is: "How do I want to die?" We give thought to so many other areas of our lives, but we seldom think of our own death, except in fear. No matter how your parents died, your leaving the planet can be a positive experience for you. How are you preparing for your death? Do you want to expire sick and helpless in a hospital bed, stuck with tubes? Or when it is your time to go, would you like to have an afternoon party for your friends, then go in to take a nap and not wake up? I definitely prefer having a party, and I am programming myself so that my life will end that way. If your current picture of dying is negative, you can always change it. We can all make dying a peaceful and joyous experience.

Planetary or global healing is a response to the awareness that what we experience in our outer world is a mirror for the energy patterns within us. An important part of any healing process is to acknowledge our connection and contribution to the whole of Life and to begin the process of projecting positive healing energy out into the world. This is a place where so many of us get stuck in our own energy, unaware of the healing power of giving and sharing. Healing is a continuous process, and if we wait until we are "healed" to begin sharing love, we may never have the opportunity to do so.

The saying, "Oh, I am too old to do this or that" will become totally outmoded as we find elders accomplishing all the things we said they couldn't. The idea of being "too old" may become something that happens only shortly before death. There is no reason we cannot be full of life until our last days.

There is a group of women in Dallas, ranging from 62 to 80, who practice karate on a regular basis. They have become a karate demonstration group called the Steele Magnolias. They go around to various centers proving that karate can be a sport for senior women. Also, these women can easily defend themselves if attacked in any situation.

There are also groups of older women around the country who get together and invest in the stock market. Some of these groups have been quite successful at it. A group in Illinois has put out a book called *The Beardstown Ladies Common Sense Investment Guide.* This book has sold over 300,000 copies.

A recent study in Pennsylvania has found that elders in their 80s and 90s who attend a weight-lifting exercise program can revitalize their bodies. They can regain control of muscles that have been dormant for years. The disability often associated with aging is really an effect of years of inactivity. The trainers learned that people in their 90s can triple their strength in less than two months. This exercise also has a stimulating effect on their minds.

We are discovering that the brain does not wither and die unless we stop using it. As long as we stimulate ourselves with mental pursuits and exercises, as long as we stay interested in life, our brains stay alert. Life becomes really dull and boring when we don't challenge our brains. How small and narrow are the lives of people who never exercise and who only talk about their illnesses.

Almost all the research done on older people has been by the pharmaceutical industry, on dis-ease, on and what is "wrong" with elders, and what drugs we require. There is a need to do in-depth studies of older people who are healthy, happy, fulfilled, and enjoying their lives. The more we study what is "right" with older people, the more we will know how we can all accomplish healthy living. Unfortunately, the pharmaceutical companies do not make money on healthy people, so they never fund studies like this.

No matter what our age or what kind of problems we have, we can begin to make positive changes today. As long as we can begin with the willingness to love and cherish ourselves, we will learn to love. As we love ourselves a little more each day, we will also be more open to love from others. The Law of Love requires that we focus our attention on what we *do* want, rather than what we *don't* want. Focus on loving *you*. Use the affirmation: *"I love myself totally in this moment."*

If we want to be respected and honored when we are older, then we must lay the groundwork by respecting and honoring the elders we meet in our lives today. How we treat elders today is the way we will be treated later. Not only do we need to listen to our elders again, we need to listen to the new emerging voice of our vital, older women. We have so much to learn from them. These women are exploding with energy, wisdom, and knowledge. They see life as a path of awakening; instead of getting old, they just keep growing.

I highly recommend the book *New Passages: Mapping Your Life Across Time,* by Gail Sheehy. Her insight into The New Map of Adult Life and the possibility of changes that lie before us has touched a place in my heart that wants to help all of us become Elders of Excellence in time. No matter how young you are, you will probably live a very long life, and now is the time to prepare for enjoyable, fulfilling later years.

A helpful way to make these positive changes is to use affirmations. While all the thoughts and words we use are affirmations, when we talk about "doing affirmations" we mean creating positive statements that consciously reprogram our minds to accept new ways of living. Choose affirmations that empower you as an elder, an Elder of Excellence. Every day affirm at least a few of these, first thing in the morning and the last thing at night. Begin and end your day on a positive note.

Affirmations for Being an *Elder of Excellence*

I have my whole life ahead of me.

I am young and beautiful...at every age.

I contribute to society in fulfilling and productive ways.

I am in charge of my finances, my health, and my future.

I am respected by all whom I come in contact with.

I honor and respect the children and adolescents in my life.

I greet each new day with energy and joy.

I live every day to the fullest.

I sleep well at night.

I think new and different thoughts each day.

My life is a glorious adventure.

I am open to experiencing all that life has to offer.

My family is supportive of me, and I am supportive of them.

I have no limitations.

I speak up; my voice is heard by the leaders in society.

I take the time to play with my inner child.

I meditate, take quiet walks, and enjoy nature; I enjoy spending time alone.

Laughter is a big part of my life; I hold nothing back.

I think of ways to help heal the planet, and I implement them.

I contribute to the harmony of life.

I have all the time in the world.

My later years are my treasure years.

A Healing Meditation

I rejoice in each passing year. My wealth of knowledge grows, and I am in touch with my wisdom. I feel the guidance of angels every step of the way. I know how to live. I know how to keep myself youthful and healthy. My body is renewed at every moment. I am vital, vivacious, healthy, fully alive, and contributing to my last day. I am at peace with my age. I create the kind of relationships I want to have. I create the prosperity I need. I know how to be triumphant. My later years are my Treasure Years, and I become an Elder of Excellence. I now contribute to life in every way I can, knowing I am love, joy, peace, and infinite wisdom now and forever more.

And so it is!

✳ ✳ ✳

✵ Chapter X ✵

Building a Financially Secure Future

Women have been so protected by the men in their lives. Men often take the attitude that women need not "disturb their pretty little heads with finances." Daddy and husband will take care of it all. That does not leave women prepared for divorce and widowhood. Our pretty little heads are more than capable of learning about money management. In grammar school and junior high, girls are almost always ahead of boys in math.

Today it is time for women to learn more about banking and investments. We are perfectly competent. Every woman needs to be financially independent, but we are seldom taught about money at home or in school. We are not taught about the world of economics. In the traditional family, the man took care of the money, and the woman took care of the children and cleaning. Many women are much more capable of handling money than men are, and some men are much more capable of handling cooking and cleaning. To say that finances belong in the world of men is just another way of keeping women in their place.

Many women are frightened of the word *finance* only because it is a new subject. I think that we have to go beyond the old thinking that women don't understand. We think that we don't know things, but we are brighter than we think we are, and we can learn. We need to take classes, listen to tapes, read books, and create study groups. When we learn more about money and the world of finance, we won't be so frightened of it.

Here in San Diego we have nonprofit groups, such as the Women's Institute for Financial Education, and Consumers Credit Counselors, who offer courses at no charge.

Most colleges and universities offer courses taught through continuing-education programs in the evenings or on weekends. These classes are aimed at helping women become more comfortable with handling money and investments. This, in turn, gives women confidence. I am sure that you will find the same sort of classes available in your area. Look for them.

All women need to understand money, finances, and investments. Even if you are a happily married woman, you love being a housewife, you love your children, and all that, you need to know these things. What if your husband suddenly dies or divorces you and you are confronted with raising children on your own? That's when women get into trouble—when they have not been educated. Learn about these subjects while you can. If you do so before you need it, maybe you'll never need to use it. Knowledge is always power.

Even if we start accumulating money at the smallest level, we can begin to move towards wealth. It is fun to see our savings increase and grow. From savings we move into investments. Then your money is working for you rather than you working for your money. For some time now, I have used the affirmation: MY INCOME IS CONSTANTLY INCREASING, AND I PROSPER WHEREVER I TURN. I have made that a personal law for myself, and you can, too. It will help to change your consciousness about money. I speak from experience because I came from poverty, real poverty. For much of my life, I didn't have any money at all. I did not have a prosperity consciousness. I had a poverty consciousness. I have come to where I am today by right of consciousness. By that I mean that my thoughts about myself, life, and money changed. As my thinking changed, my consciousness and my world changed.

I was a depression baby. Money was almost nonexistent. We had no hot water and cooked on a wood stove for all of my childhood. A refrigerator was an unheard-of luxury. My father worked in a government-supported jobs program, WPA, and earned a little money when I was small, but not much. I remember how thrilled I was when I finally received a job in the dimestore. But that was my consciousness expanding in those days. I worked in a stock room and a diner; I did all sorts of menial work because my consciousness believed that that was what I deserved. It took a long time for me to break through those beliefs. As my understanding began to grow, I was able to realize that there is an abundance in the universe. This abundance is available for those of us who will expand our consciousness. The Universe loves to give. We are the ones who have a hard time receiving. We will remain in lack until we can expand our consciousness to accept the idea that we are *allowed* to prosper, that we *deserve* to prosper, that we *can* prosper. Only then can we allow the Universe to give to us.

Most women are saying "I want money," "I need money." And yet we are doing everything we can to build walls around us so that money can't get in. The most difficult workshop you can possibly teach is a prosperity workshop. People get very, very angry when their beliefs about prosperity are challenged. And the women who are in the most need of money usually have the strongest poverty beliefs. They are also the ones who get the most irate when those beliefs are challenged. Anyone can change their limiting beliefs, but the more there is to change, the harder the process seems, and the more scared and protective you can become.

Be sure to make your list: WHAT I BELIEVE ABOUT MONEY. List all your beliefs, every remark you heard as a child about money, work, earnings, and prosperity. Also write down how you feel about money. Do you hate money? Is it filthy? Do you crumple it when it comes your way? Have you ever spoken lovingly to a $10 bill? Do you bless your bills when they come in? Do you ever thank the phone company for giving you service and trusting you to pay your bill? Are you grateful when you do get money, or do you always complain that it is not enough? Really look at your attitude toward and with money! You may be surprised by what you find.

When I first started bringing money into my life that was above the subsistence level, I used to feel very, very guilty about it. I would try to give it away or I would spend it on foolish things so that I could be broke again. Having some extra money was so contrary to my early belief systems that on a subconscious level I had to get rid of it. It took me a long time to change my beliefs and know that I deserved to make, enjoy, and save money.

Women need to understand that nothing comes into our lives until we have created it in consciousness, and therefore we have already earned it—earned it by right of consciousness. We put mental contributions (positive affirmations) into our cosmic bank. When we have deposited enough of them, they come back to us in the form of prosperity. Don't feel guilty about bringing good into your life. You've already earned it! You don't have to pay for it; you've already done your work. That's why it's here.

When your income starts to increase, when your work gets better, when the money starts pouring in, you've already earned it in consciousness. This new state is yours to enjoy. So a good affirmation to use would be: I'VE ALREADY EARNED THIS. I DESERVE IT. I'VE ALREADY EARNED IT. Then be thankful and grateful. As I said before, the Universe loves a grateful person.

Don't waste time wondering why you may be prosperous when other women are not. We all operate under the law of our own consciousness. Everyone else has the ability to create good in their lives as soon as they open their consciousness to new ideas. Spiritual awakening is always here for us; it is up to us to be willing. Opportunity is always available; whether we accept it or not is up to us. When the student is ready, the teacher appears—not a moment before and not a moment later.

I believe in tithing to yourself. It is a very powerful thing to do. Tithing to yourself is saying to the Universe: "I am worthy, I deserve, I accept." I suggest that women tithe between 10 and 20 percent of their earnings to themselves. Take it off the top of your income. This money is not to be used for day-to-day things. It is to be saved and only used to make major purchases such as a home or business. This keeps you from dipping into these earnings. Even if you start out with small amounts, start putting money away. It's amazing how fast it adds up. Tithing to yourself is an act of self-love and helps to create self-worth.

The churches want you to tithe only to God, by way of donations to their church. But you are part of God. You are a part of All That Is. Tithe to your spiritual source if you want to, but also tithe to yourself. And don't make the mistake of waiting to tithe until you earn more. With that poverty thinking, you will never earn enough to tithe. You have to take a leap of faith now and take this money off the top, before you even get it in your hands to spend. Then you can budget with the amount that is left. It's amazing how this exercise brings more good into your life. Tithing to yourself is like creating a money magnet!

✷ Chapter XI ✷

Women in Support of Women

An "Empowering Women" support group can be a focused opportunity for women to identify their limiting beliefs through practicing a variety of exercises, using affirmations to change old beliefs, enjoying the marvelous changes in their lives, and sharing the process with others. The group process offers wonderful energy to support change.

You do not need to be perfect to organize an Empowering Women group. However, you *do* need to use these ideas and principles in your own life, have a desire to share this information with others, and have an open heart and a willingness to listen. Leading a group is a growth process for the leader as well as the participants, so expect that some of "your stuff" will be triggered. How wonderful! It is all an opportunity to continue the healing and growing processes. Remember that loving yourself and loving others are the most important tasks we have on this planet.

An Empowering Women support group can be a casual get-together of several women friends, perhaps on a weekly basis. The group sessions could be based on the chapters in this book. Each week you may wish to discuss a different chapter. Other resources you may find useful are my other books, including *You Can Heal Your Life* and *Life! Reflections on Your Journey*.

Don't use a support group as a reason to sit around in a group and play "ain't it awful." Instead, use the group as a stepping-stone in your growth process. It does no good to support old patterns and see who has the worst life this week. Use the group to support positive change.

General Guidelines

One of the first and most important exercises is to find out WHAT you believe. This can be a real eye opener. Put several full sheets of paper in your notebook, and label each one at the top: WHAT I BELIEVE ABOUT...

- Men
- Women
- Myself
- Relationships
- Commitment
- Marriage
- Family
- Children
- Work
- Money
- Prosperity
- Investments
- Health
- Aging
- Death

These beliefs are the internal, subconscious rules you live your life by. You cannot make positive changes in your life until you can recognize the negative beliefs you hold.

When all of the lists are more or less completed, read them over.

Mark with a star each belief that is nourishing and supportive of you. These beliefs are the ones you want to keep and reinforce.

Mark with a check each belief that is negative and detrimental to your goals. These are the beliefs that have been holding you back from being all that you can be. These are the beliefs you want to erase and reprogram.

You might want to add more subjects. You might want to work on one subject a week, giving each person time to discuss their lists.

Here are some suggestions for those who want to start a support group:

1. Create a space that is safe for deep sharing. Ways to do this include asking everyone to make a commitment to confidentiality, sharing some of your own processes, and making it clear that the group is a place to let down the masks we often wear. No one is expected to have a "perfect" life. The group is about learning new ways to deal with the issues in our lives. The meeting place can be your living room, a conference room, or a church.
2. Cultivate a nonjudgmental, accepting attitude. Do not tell anyone what they "should" do. Offer suggestions for ways they could change their thoughts and perspectives. If people sense judgment, they

will immediately go into resistance.

3. Center yourself before each group session. Use affirmations such as: *"Spirit guides my thoughts, words, and actions throughout each session,"* and *"I trust the Divine Wisdom within me as I lead the group."* If something challenging happens during the group, immediately take a deep breath and think a positive affirmation.
4. At the beginning of the group, you can suggest the following:
   - Be on time!
   - Make a commitment to attend all sessions. Continuity is important.
   - Listen attentively, and respect each woman's sharing.
   - Do NOT cross-talk while someone is speaking.
   - Ask everyone for a commitment to confidentiality for issues shared in the group. It's important that participants feel safe when they share.
   - Focus sharing on the issue, not

the whole "story."

- Use "I" statements such as "I feel..." rather than "They made me..."
- Be respectful of the time, and the need to give others a chance to share.

5. It's important for everyone to have some time to share during each session. If the group is large, you can have people form small groups of five or six for an exercise or for sharing.
6. Occasionally, there will be someone in the group who is very talkative or in some way disruptive. Recognize that someone who is trying to dominate the group is acting out of her own fear of not being good enough or not getting enough attention. It is best to talk with this woman after the group, in an individual setting. You might say in a loving way, "I appreciate that you have a lot to share with the group. My concern is that others who are not as assertive may feel inhibited. Next week, could you be conscious of letting others speak, and let them share first? Thank you." Finding

some task that this woman could assist you with may also be helpful.

7. Experiential work is a most important method of awareness. In each group session, offer an experiential exercise such as mirror work, inner child meditation, "should" exercises, and so on.
8. Be flexible. With the group process, you may not always get through everything you had planned. Since Divine Right Action is always happening, learn to trust the process and it will flow!
9. Frequently monitor yourself and your reactions. If you begin to feel anxious or inadequate, take a few deep breaths, relax, and silently say a positive affirmation.
10. Don't argue with someone who seems to want to stay stuck. Try not to allow yourself to become depressed by someone else's drama. As the group leader, you must learn to hold on to that sense of KNOWING that healing is available for everyone, regardless of external circumstances. The TRUTH is that Spirit is more powerful than dis-ease, financial challenge, or relationship issues!

11. Develop a sense of humor! Laughter is a marvelous way of gaining a different perspective.
12. Women in the group will often have some very deep emotions that they need to express and release. It's important that you be able to handle the expression of grief, anger, and rage if you want to help others release them. If you find yourself fearful of deep emotions, you may want to find a therapist whom you trust to help you explore the fear.
13. After each group session, go to the mirror and tell yourself how well you're doing, especially if you are new to leading groups.
14. Begin and end your groups with a meditation or centering process. It can be as simple as having everyone close their eyes and breathe for a moment or two. I like to have everyone hold hands. I ask them to feel the energy in the hands next to theirs. Then I remind them that everyone in that room wants the same things that they want. Each woman wants to be healthy, to be prosperous, to give and

receive love, and to express herself creatively in ways that are fulfilling to her. During the closing meditation, I remind them that each one of us, myself included, has learned something that will improve the quality of our lives. All is well, and we are safe.

15. Each group is different, and each session will be different. Learn to flow with the energy of the current group and session.
16. For each session, you will need:
    - A cassette player for playing meditation tapes and music
    - A hand-held mirror and/or full-length mirror
    - Paper and pens
    - Several boxes of tissues
    - Candles or incense (optional) to create a sacred atmosphere
17. Ask participants to bring a journal for writing and a hand mirror to each session. They may also want to bring a pillow for sitting or for use during meditations, and a stuffed animal for hugging!

✳ ✳ ✳

✵ Conclusion ✵

We all think that we have so many problems. Yet all these problems fall under just four categories of life: love, health, prosperity, and self-expression. So, in spite of how overwhelming it all looks, we only have four areas to clean up. And love is the most important of all. When we love ourselves, it is easy to love others and for others to love us. This, in turn, improves our relationships and our work conditions. Loving ourselves is the key ingredient for good health. Love of self and love of life connects us with the prosperity of the Universe. Self-love creates self-expression and allows us to be creative in deeply fulfilling ways.

We Are All Pioneers!

I personally feel that every woman is a pioneer today. Early pioneer women blazed trails. They took risks. They dealt with loneliness and fear. They lived lives of poverty and hardship. They had to help build their own shelters and forage for their own food. Even if they were married, their men were often away for long periods of time. Women had to fend for themselves and their children. They had to find their own resources. And they laid the groundwork for settling this country. The men would never have made America what it is today without those courageous women.

Today's pioneer women are like you and me. We have incredible opportunities to fulfill ourselves and to bring about equality between the sexes. We want to bloom where we are planted and make life better for all women. If Life is pushing women to a new level of achievement and freedom, then there must be a reason for it. We must find out how to take advantage of this cycle. We need new maps for living. Society is moving into uncharted waters. We are just beginning to learn what sorts of things we can accomplish. So grab your compass and come along. We all have much to learn and much to give. We can all be map makers and pacesetters, no matter what part of society we come from.

We are born alone and we die alone. We choose how to fill the spaces in between. There is no limit to our creativity or our possibilities. We want to find joy in our capabilities. So many of us were raised to believe we couldn't take care of ourselves. It feels great to know we can. We need to say to ourselves often, "Whatever happens, I know I can handle it."

From the level of emotional maturity, women are at their highest point in their evolution in this lifetime. We are now the best we have ever been. So this is the perfect time for us to shape our own destiny. The advances we make now will set a new standard for women everywhere. There are many possibilities in life beyond what we may presently think or experience. We now have opportunities never available to women before. It is time to connect with other women, to improve life for all women. This will, in turn, improve life for men. When women are fulfilled, satisfied and happy, they will, be wonderful partners, wonderful people to work with and to live with. And men will feel infinitely more comfortable with equals!

We must work to strengthen the ties between women, to support each other in our paths of growth. We have no time now to play the old competition game with other women over men. Females are coming into their own. We want to learn all that we can so that we can pass this strength and power on to our children and our children's children. Then, women will never again have to go through all the diminishment and abuse that *we* have gone through, and that our mothers and grandmothers and their grandmothers endured. We can only accomplish this new freedom and acknowledgment by working together to bring women into their own.

Love Yourself, and Love Your Life!

✵ ✵ ✵ ✵ ✵ ✵

❋ ❋ ❋

Inside of you is a smart,

powerful, dynamic,

capable, self-confident

alive, alert, fabulous

woman.

Let her come out

and play.

The world is waiting

for you.

❋ ❋ ❋

APPENDIX

SELF-HELP RESOURCES

The following list of resources can be used for more information about recovery options for issues surrounding addictions, health concerns, death and bereavement, or problems related to dysfunctional families. The addresses and telephone numbers listed are for the national headquarters; look in your local yellow pages under "Community Services" for resources closer to your area.

In addition to the following groups, other self-help organizations may be available in your area to assist your healing and recovery for a particular life crisis not listed here. Consult your telephone directory, call a counseling center or help line near you, or write or call:

American Self-Help Clearinghouse
St. Clares-Riverside
Medical Center
Denville, NJ 07834
(201) 625-7101

National Self-Help Clearinghouse
25 West 43rd St.,
Room 620
New York, NY 10036
(212) 642-2944

AIDS

AIDS Hotline
(800) 342-2437

Children with AIDS Project of America
4020 N. 20th St., Ste. 101
Phoenix, AZ 85016
(602) 265-4859
Hotline
(602) 843-8654

The Names Project — AIDS Quilt
(800) 872-6263

National AIDS Network
(800) 342-2437

Project Inform
19655 Market St.,
Ste. 220
San Francisco, CA 94103
(415) 558-8669

PWA Coalition
50 W. 17th St.
New York, NY 10011

Spanish AIDS Hotline
(800) 344-7432

TDD (Hearing Impaired) AIDS Hotline
(800) 243-7889

ALCOHOL ABUSE

Al-Anon Family Headquarters
200 Park Ave. South
New York, NY 10003
(804) 563-1600

Alcoholics Anonymous (AA)
General Service Office
475 Riverside Dr.
New York, NY 10115
(212) 870-3400

Children of Alcoholics Foundation
P.O. Box 4185
Grand Central Station
New York, NY
10163-4185
(212) 754-0656
(800) 359-COAF

Meridian Council, Inc.
Administrative Offices
4 Elmcrest Terrace
Norwalk, CT 06850

National Association of Children of Alcoholics (NACOA)
11426 Rockville Pike,
Ste. 100
Rockville, MD 20852
(301) 468-0985

National Clearinghouse for Alcohol and Drug Information (NCADI)
P.O. Box 234
Rockville, MD 20852
(301) 468-2600

National Council on Alcoholism and Drug Dependency (NCADD)
12 West 21st St.
New York, NY 10010
(212) 206-6770

ANOREXIA/ BULIMIA

American Anorexia/Bulimia Association, Inc.
293 Central Park West, Ste. 1R
New York, NY 10024
(212) 501-8351

Eating Disorder Organization
1925 East Dublin Granville Rd.
Columbus, OH 43229-3517
(918) 481-4044

CANCER

National Cancer Institute
(800) 4-CANCER

ECAP (Exceptional Cancer Patients)
Bernie S. Siegel, M.D.
300 Plaza Middlesex
Middletown, CT 06457
(860) 343-5950

CHILDREN'S ISSUES

Child Molestation

Adults Molested As Children United (AMACU)
232 East Gish Rd.
San Jose, CA 95112
(800) 422-4453

National Committee for Prevention of Child Abuse
332 South Michigan Ave., Ste. 1600
Chicago, IL 60604
(312) 663-3520

Children's and Teens' Crisis Intervention

Boy's Town Crisis Hotline
(800) 448-3000

Covenant House Hotline
(800) 999-9999

Kid Save
(800) 543-7283

National Runaway and Suicide Hotline
(800) 621-4000

Missing Children

Missing Children-Help Center
410 Ware Blvd., Ste. 400
Tampa, FL 33619
(800) USA-KIDS

National Center for Missing and Exploited Children
1835 K St. NW
Washington, DC 20006
(800) 843-5678

Terminally Ill Children (Fulfilling Wishes)

Brass Ring Society
(918) 743-3232

CO-DEPENDENCY

Co-Dependents Anonymous
60 E. Richards Way
Sparks, NV 89431
(602) 277-7991

DEATH/ GRIEVING/ SUICIDE

Grief Recovery Helpline
(800) 445-4808

Grief Recovery Institute
8306 Wilshire Blvd., Ste. 21A
Beverly Hills, CA 90211
(213) 650-1234

Mothers Against Drunk Driving (MADD)
(817) 690-6233

National Hospice Organization (NHO)
1901 Moore St., #901
Arlington, VA 22209
(703) 243-5900

National Sudden Infant Death Syndrome
Two Metro Plaza, Ste. 205
Landover, MD 20785
(800) 221-SIDS

Seasons: Suicide Bereavement
4777 Naniola Dr.
Salt Lake City, UT 84117

DEBTS

Debtors Anonymous
General Service Office
P.O. Box 400
Grand Central Station
New York, NY
10163-0400
(212) 642-8220

DIABETES

American Diabetes Association
(800) 232-3472

DRUG ABUSE

Cocaine Anonymous
(800) 347-8998

National Cocaine-Abuse Hotline
(800) 262-2463
(800) COCAINE

National Institute of Drug Abuse (NIDA)
Parklawn Building
5600 Fishers Lane,
Room 10A-39
Rockville, MD 20852
(301) 443-6245 (for information)
(800) 662-4357 (for help)

World Service Office (CA)
3740 Overland Ave., #C
Los Angeles, CA
90034-6337
(310) 559-5833

EATING DISORDERS

Overeaters Anonymous
National Office
Rio Rancho, NM
(505) 891-2664

Eating Disorder Organization
1925 East Dublin Granville Rd.
Columbus, OH 43229-3517
(918) 481-4044

GAMBLING

Gamblers Anonymous
National Council on Compulsive Gambling
444 West 59th St., Room 1521
New York, NY 10019
(212) 903-4400

HEALTH ISSUES

Alzheimer's Disease Information
(800) 621-0379

American Chronic Pain Association
P.O. Box 850
Rocklin, CA 95677
(916) 632-0922

American Foundation of Traditional Chinese Medicine
1280 Columbus Ave., Ste. 302
San Francisco, CA 94133
(415) 776-0502

American Holistic Health Association
P.O. Box 17400
Anaheim, CA 92817
(714) 779-6152

Chopra Center for Well-Being
Deepak Chopra, M.D.
7630 Fay Ave.
La Jolla, CA 92037
(619) 551-7788

The Fetzer Institute
9292 West KL Ave.
Kalamazoo, MI 49009
(616) 375-2000

Hippocrates Health Institute
1443 Palmdale Court
West Palm Beach, FL 33411
(407) 471-8876

Hospicelink
(800) 331-1620

Institute for Noetic Sciences
P.O. Box 909, Dept. M
Sausalito, CA 94966-0909
(800) 383-1394

The Mind-Body Medical Institute
185 Pilgrim Rd.
Boston, MA 02215
(617) 632-9525

National Health Information Center
P.O. Box 1133
Washington, DC 20013-1133
(800) 336-4797

Optimum Health Care Institute
6970 Central Ave.
Lemon Grove, CA 91945
(619) 464-3346

Preventive Medicine Research Institute
Dean Ornish, M.D.
900 Bridgeway, Ste. 2
Sausalito, CA 94965
(415) 332-2525

World Research Foundation
20501 Ventura Blvd., Ste. 100
Woodland Hills, CA 91364
(818) 999-5483

INCEST

Incest Survivors Resource Network International, Inc.
P.O. Box 7375
Las Cruces, NM 88006-7375
(505) 521-4260

PET BEREAVEMENT

Bide-A-Wee Foundation
New York, NY
(212) 532-6395

The Animal Medical Center
510 E. 62nd St.
New York, NY 10021
(212) 838-8100

Holistic Animal Consulting Center
29 Lyman Ave.
Staten Island, NY 10305
(718) 720-5548

RAPE

Austin Rape Crisis Center
1824 East Oltorf
Austin, TX 78741
(512) 440-7273

SEX ADDICTIONS

National Council on Sexual Addictions
P.O. Box 652
Azle, TX 76098-0652
(800) 321-2066

SMOKING ABUSE

Nicotine Anonymous
2118 Greenwich St.
San Francisco, CA 94123
(415) 750-0328

SPOUSAL ABUSE

National Coalition Against Domestic Violence
P.O. Box 34103
Washington, DC
20043-4103
(202) 638-6388

National Domestic Violence Hotline
(800) 799-SAFE

STRESS REDUCTION

The Biofeedback & Psychophysiology Clinic
The Menninger Clinic
P.O. Box 829
Topeka, KS 66601-0829
(913) 350-5000

New York Open Center
(In-depth workshops to invigorate the spirit)
83 Spring St.
New York, NY 10012
(212) 219-2527

Omega Institute
(A healing, spiritual retreat community)
260 Lake Dr.
Rhinebeck, NY 12572-3212
(914) 266-4444 (info)
(800) 944-1001 (to enroll)

Rise Institute
P.O. Box 2733
Petaluma, CA 94973
(707) 765-2758

The Stress Reduction Clinic
Jon Kabat-Zinn, Ph.D.
University of Massachusetts Medical Center
55 Lake Avenue North
Worcester, MA 01655
(508) 856-1616
(508) 856-2656

RECOMMENDED BOOKS AND AUDIOS BY EMPOWERED WOMEN

Anatomy of the Spirit: The Seven Stages of Power and Healing
— Caroline Myss, Ph.D.

Confidence: Finding It and Living It
— Barbara De Angelis, Ph.D.

Cooking for Healthy Healing
— Linda G. Rector-Page, N.D., Ph.D.

Do What You Love, the Money Will Follow
— Marsha Sinetar

Feel the Fear and Do It Anyway
— Susan Jeffers, Ph.D.

A God Who Looks Like Me
— Patricia Lynn Reilly

Great American Cookbook
— Marilyn Diamond

Growing Older, Growing Better
— Amy E. Dean

Healthy Healing, An Alternative Healing Reference
— Linda G. Rector-Page, N.D., Ph.D.

The Heroic Path: One Woman's Journey from Cancer to Self-Healing
— Angela Passidomo Trafford

"I'd Change My Life If I Had More Time"
— Doreen Virtue, Ph.D.

Lighten Up (audiocassette)
— Carol Hansen (Open Heart Productions: 510-974-9088)

The Menopause Industry: How the Medical Establishment Exploits Women
— Sandra Coney

New Passages: Mapping Your Life Across Time
— Gail Sheehy

Reinventing Womanhood
— Carolyn Heilbrun

Take Back Your Power: A Working Woman's Response to Sexual Harassment
— Jennifer Coburn

The Western Guide to Feng Shui
— Terah Kathryn Collins

What Every Woman Needs to Know Before (and After) She Gets Involved with Men and Money
— Judge Lois Forer

Woman Heal Thyself: An Ancient Healing System for Contemporary Woman
— Jeanne Elizabeth Blum

A Woman's Worth
— Marianne Williamson

Women Alone: Creating a Joyous and Fulfilling Life
— Julie Keene and Ione Jenson

Women's Bodies, Women's Wisdom
(as well as her audios and newsletters)
— Christiane Northrup, M.D.

Women Who Love Too Much
— Robin Norwood

✵ About the Author ✵

LOUISE L. HAY is a metaphysical lecturer and teacher and the bestselling author of 18 books, including ***You Can Heal Your Life*** and ***Life! Reflections on Your Journey***. Her works have been translated into 25 different languages in 33 countries throughout the world. Since beginning her career as a Science of Mind minister in 1981, Louise has assisted thousands of people in discovering and using the full potential of their own creative powers for personal growth and self-healing. Louise is the owner and founder of Hay House, Inc., a self-help publishing company that disseminates books and audios that contribute to the healing of the planet.